Shame
To
Miss

3

Poetry collections by Anne Fine published by Corgi Books:

A SHAME TO MISS . . . 1

A SHAME TO MISS . . . 2

A SHAME TO MISS . . . 3

Published by Doubleday for older readers:

UP ON CLOUD NINE

'A real treat for the many fans of the Children's Laureate; a highly enjoyable
novel that is characteristically funny, clever and moving' *Financial Times*

Other books by Anne Fine for older readers:

THE SUMMER-HOUSE LOON

THE OTHER DARKER NED

THE STONE MENAGERIE

ROUND BEHIND THE ICEHOUSE

THE GRANNY PROJECT

MADAME DOUBTFIRE

GOGGLE-EYES

THE BOOK OF THE BANSHEE

FLOUR BABIES

STEP BY WICKED STEP

THE TULIP TOUCH

Published by Doubleday/Yearling for junior readers:

CHARM SCHOOL

'A funny read which pre-teens should latch on to' *Children's Bookseller*

BAD DREAMS

'A beautifully plotted, well-told mix of fantasy thriller and closely observed
school drama' *Daily Telegraph*

www.annefine.co.uk

A Shame To Miss 3

SELECTED BY

ANNE FINE

Corgi Books

www.annefine.co.uk

A SHAME TO MISS . . . 3
A CORGI BOOK 0 552 548693

Published in Great Britain by Corgi Books,
an imprint of Random House Children's Books

This edition published 2002

1 3 5 7 9 10 8 6 4 2

Compilation and introduction copyright © Anne Fine, 2002

The Acknowledgements on page 167 constitute an extension of this
copyright notice.

Set in Palatino

Corgi Books are published by Random House Children's Books,
61–63 Uxbridge Road, London W5 5SA
a division of The Random House Group Ltd,
in Australia by Random House Australia (Pty) Ltd,
20 Alfred Street, Milsons Point, Sydney, NSW 2061, Australia,
in New Zealand by Random House New Zealand Ltd,
18 Poland Road, Glenfield, Auckland 10, New Zealand,
and in South Africa by Random House (Pty) Ltd,
Endulini, 5A Jubilee Road, Parktown 2193, South Africa

THE RANDOM HOUSE GROUP Limited Reg. No. 954009

www.**kids**at**random**house.co.uk

A CIP catalogue record for this book is available from the British Library.

Typeset by SX Composing DTP, Rayleigh, Essex
Printed and bound in Great Britain by
Bookmarque Ltd, Croydon, Surrey

Contents

For Richard

Introduction

What I've done here is pick the poems young people seem to like best. Show the collection to adults and half will be stabbing the odd page muttering, 'This one's a bit unsuitable, isn't it?' and the other half will be reeling round the room clutching their heads, wailing, 'What, only one Keats sonnet? Only *one*?'

Ignore them. See what you think. Remember that some of the more old-fashioned poems are easier to enjoy if you decode them first. Take Wordsworth's 'On Westminster Bridge':

Earth has not anything to show more fair:
Dull would he be of soul who could pass by
A sight so touching in its majesty:
This City now . . .

Translate that into, say,

Champion view!
You'd have to be a stone to walk past that.
Breaks your heart, dunnit,
London . . .

and you'll begin to see why Wordsworth has the edge on the average hungover dawn homegoer leaning over a parapet.

You read a poem. Some images and phrases stick, and from that moment you can see flashes of the world through that poet's eyes. Practically every adult you know says every November, 'It's getting dark so *early*.' You don't think twice about it. Then you read E. J. Scovell –

The days fail. Night broods over afternoon.

– and the poet's way of putting it haunts you. You see what's happening in a richer way. In her autobiography *To the Island*, Janet Frame describes the magical effect of her private reading at this age as:

. . . the other world's arrival in my world – the literature streaming through it like an array of beautiful ribbons through the branches of a green growing tree, touching the leaves with unexpected light.

One thing to bear in mind is that you often don't fully 'get' a poem until a long time after you first come across it. You may study or even learn it by heart – usually because someone makes you. But only when you fall in – or out   of love, lose someone, travel, can't sleep for a week, stand in a snowstorm, get bitten by a dog or whatever, do the chosen words spring to mind. Now you can truly understand how brilliantly the experience was captured.

So try to think of some poems as having, like flu medicines, a kind of timed release. Take even those on trust. I promise you, you won't be sorry later.

Anne Fine

A Class-room

The day was wide and that whole room was wide,
The sun slanting across the desks, the dust
Of chalk rising. I was listening
As if for the first time,
As if I'd never heard our tongue before,
As if a music came alive for me.
And so it did upon the lift of language,
A battle poem, *Lepanto*. In my blood
The high call stirred and brimmed.
I was possessed yet coming for the first
Time into my own
Country of green and sunlight,
Place of harvest and waiting
Where the corn would never all be garnered but
Leave in the sun always at least one swathe.
So from a battle I learnt this healing peace,
Language a spell over the hungry dreams,
A password and a key. That day is still
Locked in my mind. When poetry is spoken
That door is opened and the light is shed,
The gold of language tongued and minted fresh.
And later I began to use my words,
Stared into verse within that class-room and
Was called at last only by kind inquiry
'How old are you?' 'Thirteen.'
'You are a thinker.' More than thought it was
That caught me up excited, charged and changed,
Made ready for the next fine spell of words,
Locked into language with a golden key.

Elizabeth Jennings

A Slice of Wedding Cake

Why have such scores of lovely, gifted girls
   Married impossible men?
Simple self-sacrifice may be ruled out,
   And missionary endeavour, nine times out of ten.

Repeat 'impossible men'; not merely rustic,
   Foul-tempered or depraved
(Dramatic foils chosen to show the world
   How well women behave, and always have behaved).

Impossible men: idle, illiterate,
   Self-pitying, dirty, sly,
For whose appearance even in City parks
   Excuses must be made to casual passers-by.

Has God's supply of tolerable husbands
   Fallen, in fact, so low?
Or do I always over-value woman
   At the expense of man?
                Do I?
                    It might be so.

Robert Graves

Sonnet

Hold both my hands. Be careful of the pins.
My mother's making candles from my nails.
She's blocked the outside drain with wedding veils.
I smile at all the crooning wheelie bins;
I'm filleting silk fish with amber fins.
My twenty ships, rigged with macramé sails,
are taking tests which every zebra fails
and winning oranges from metal twins.

Tomorrow, I will make a loaf of bread
from coloured glass and smoke and PVC
and five dead flowers and my income tax.

I'll let you have the passkey to my head.
Watch out for flowerpots that look like me.
Stick shrieking bubble gum in all the cracks.

Adèle Geras

Nora Criona

I have looked him round and looked him through,
Know everything that he will do

In such a case and such a case;
And when a frown comes on his face

I dream of it, and when a smile
I trace its sources in a while.

He cannot do a thing but I
Peep to find the reason why;

For I love him and I seek
Every evening in the week,

To peep behind his frowning eye
With little query, little pry,

And make him, if a woman can,
Happier than any man.

– Yesterday he gripped her tight
And cut her throat. And serve her right!

James Stephens

Little Elegy

(For a child who skipped rope)

Here lies resting, out of breath,
Out of turns, Elizabeth
Whose quicksilver toes not quite
Cleared the whirring edge of night.

Earth whose circles round us skim
Till they catch the lightest limb,
Shelter now Elizabeth
And for her sake trip up death.

X. J. Kennedy

from *On the Backstep of Evening*

III

You have taken away my Sundays
and given me Saturdays in exchange,
turned Mondays into Fridays,
made Thursdays rich and strange.
My Tuesdays seem like Wednesdays,
all this you have arranged,
turning weak days into strong days
with love that does not change.

Jim Greenhalf

Azrael

Who chooses the music, turns the page,
Waters the geraniums on the window-ledge?
Who proxies my hand,
Puts on the mourning ring in lieu of the diamond?

Who winds the trudging clock, who tears
Flimsy the empty date off calendars?
Who widow-hoods my senses
Lest they should meet the morning's cheat defenceless?

Who valets me at nightfall, undresses me of another day,
Puts it tidily and finally away,
And lets in darkness
To befriend my eyelids like an illusory caress?

I called him Sorrow when first he came,
But Sorrow is too narrow a name;
And though he has attended me all this long while
Habit will not do. Habit is servile.
He, inaudible, governs my days, impalpable,
Impels my hither and thither. I am his to command,
My times are in his hand.
Once in a dream I called him Azrael.

Sylvia Townsend Warner

Epitaph

They hanged him on a clement morning, swung
between the falling sunlight and the women's
breathing, like a black apostrophe to pain.
All morning while the children hushed
their hopscotch joy and the cane kept growing
he hung there sweet and low.
                        At least that's how
they tell it. It was long ago
and what can we recall of a dead slave or two
except that when we punctuate our island tale
they swing like sighs across the brutal
sentences, and anger pauses
till they pass away.

Dennis Scott

Journey of the Magi

'A cold coming we had of it,
Just the worst time of the year
For a journey, and such a long journey:
The ways deep and the weather sharp,
The very dead of winter.'
And the camels galled, sore-footed, refractory,
Lying down in the melting snow.
There were times we regretted
The summer palaces on slopes, the terraces,
And the silken girls bringing sherbert.
Then the camel men cursing and grumbling
And running away, and wanting their liquor and women,
And the night-fires going out, and the lack of shelters,
And the cities hostile and the towns unfriendly
And the villages dirty and charging high prices:
A hard time we had of it.
At the end we preferred to travel all night,
Sleeping in snatches,
With the voices singing in our ears, saying
That this was all folly.
Then at dawn we came down to a temperate valley,
Wet, below the snow line, smelling of vegetation;
With a running stream and a water-mill beating the
    darkness,
And three trees on the low sky.
And an old white horse galloped away in the meadow.
Then we came to a tavern with vine-leaves over the lintel,
Six hands at an open door dicing for pieces of silver,
And feet kicking the empty wine-skins.
But there was no information, and so we continued
And arrived at evening, not a moment too soon
Finding the place; it was (you may say) satisfactory.

All this was a long time ago, I remember,
And I would do it again, but set down
This set down
This: were we led all that way for
Birth or Death? There was a Birth, certainly,
We had evidence and no doubt. I had seen birth and death,
But had thought they were different; this Birth was
Hard and bitter agony for us, like Death, our death.
We returned to our places, these Kingdoms,
But no longer at ease here, in the old dispensation,
With an alien people clutching their gods.
I should be glad of another death.

T. S. Eliot

The Magi

Imagine this, you who have charts and maps,
guidebooks and satellites to plot your routes,
experts, advisers on the many traps
gaping for travellers, phrasebooks in the flutes
and trills of foreign tongues, rates of exchange,
inoculations to preserve your health,
search parties should you vanish out of range,
consuls to bring you home, sponsors with wealth,
websites to show you how, the Tourist Boards
eager to smooth your path, global TV,
insurance policies, the package hordes
lured by the brochures' bland security.

Imagine this: we did not know how far,
or where, what tongue, what cost, what ills, what wraith
of madness was attendant on that star.
But still we journeyed on: an act of faith.

D. A. Prince

'I see'd her in de Springtime'

I see'd her in de Springtime,
I see'd her in de Fall,
I see'd her in de Cotton patch,
A cameing from de Ball.

She hug me, an' she kiss me,
She wrung my han' an' cried.
She said I wus de sweetes' thing
Dat ever lived or died.

She hug me an' she kiss me.
Oh Heaben! De touch o' her han'!
She said I was de puttiest thing
In de shape o' mortal man.

I told her dat I love her,
Dat my love wus bed-cord strong;
Den I axed her w'en she'd have me,
An' she jes say 'Go long!'

Traditional

Song of the Battery Hen

We can't grumble about accommodation:
we have a new concrete floor that's
always dry, four walls that are
painted white, and a sheet-iron roof
the rain drums on. A fan blows warm air
beneath our feet to disperse the smell
of chicken-shit and, on dull days,
fluorescent lighting sees us.

You can tell me: if you come by
the North door, I am in the twelfth pen
on the left-hand side of the third row
from the floor; and in that pen
I am usually the middle one of three.
But, even without directions, you'd
discover me. I have the same orange-
red comb, yellow beak and auburn
feathers, but as the door opens and you
hear above the electric fan a kind of
one-word wail, I am the one
who sounds loudest in my head.

Listen. Outside this house there's an
orchard with small moss-green apple
trees; beyond that, two fields of
cabbages; then, on the far side of
the road, a broiler house. Listen:

one cockerel grows out of there, as
tall and proud as the first hour of sun.
Sometimes I stop calling with the others
to listen, and wonder if he hears me.

The next time you come here, look for me.
Notice the way I sound inside my head.
God made us all quite differently,
and blessed us with this expensive home.

Edwin Brock

from *Last Poems*

Her strong enchantments failing,
    Her towers of fear in wreck,
Her limbecks dried of poisons
    And the knife at her neck,

The Queen of air and darkness
    Begins to shrill and cry,
'O young man, O my slayer,
    To-morrow you shall die.'

O Queen of air and darkness,
    I think 'tis truth you say,
And I shall die tomorrow;
    But you will die today.

A. E. Housman

Loss

And so the game ends in this rumpled bed.
Love has been shared, the long-held hopes confessed,
The privacies explored. In our post-coital rest
He quietly snores. All mystery is dead,
The sweet, uncertain magic gone. I know
He works for Scottish Gas and has false teeth
Due to a Rugby mishap, playing Leith;
The Argyll socks conceal a hammer toe,
His widowed mother lives in Pittenweem.
He loves me. That's the worst. I can't betray
His dreadful trust, though it has swept away
The unrequited romance of my dream.
The trap has sprung. It caught my wild ideal
And there he lies, abominably real.

Alison Prince

The Rolling English Road

Before the Roman came to Rye or out to Severn strode,
The rolling English drunkard made the rolling English road.
A reeling road, a rolling road, that rambles round the shire,
And after him the parson ran, the sexton and the squire;
A merry road, a mazy road, and such as we did tread
The night we went to Birmingham by way of Beachy Head.

I knew no harm of Boneparte and plenty of the squire,
And for to fight the Frenchman I did not much desire;
But I did bash their baggonets because they came array'd
To straighten out the crooked road an English drunkard
    made,
Where you and I went down the lane with ale-mugs in
    our hands,
The night we went to Glastonbury by way of Goodwin
    Sands.

His sins they were forgiven him; or why do flowers run
Behind him; and the hedges all strengthening in the sun?
The wild thing went from left to right and knew not
    which was which,
But the wild rose was above him when they found him in
    the ditch.
God pardon us, nor harden us; we did not see so clear
That night we went to Bannockburn by way of Brighton Pier.

My friends, we will not go again or ape an ancient rage,
Or stretch the folly of our youth to be the shame of age,
But walk with clearer eyes this path that wandereth,
And see undrugged in evening light the decent inn of death;
For there is good news yet to hear, and fine things to be seen,
Before we go to Paradise by way of Kensal Green.

G. K. Chesterton

Lines upon Leaving a Sanitarium

Self-contemplation is a curse
That makes an old confusion worse.

Recumbency is unrefined
And leads to errors in the mind.

Long gazing at the ceiling will
In time induce a mental ill.

The mirror tells some truth, but not
Enough to merit constant thought.

He who himself begins to loathe
Grows sick in flesh and spirit both.

Dissection is a virtue when
It operates on other men.

Theodore Roethke

Impromptu

Keep away from sharp swords,
Don't go near a lovely woman.
A sharp sword too close will wound your hand.
Woman's beauty too close will wound your life.
The danger of the road is not in the distance,
Ten yards is far enough to break a wheel.
The peril of love is not in loving too often.
A single evening can leave its wound in the soul.

Meng Chiao

Ozymandias of Egypt

I met a traveller from an antique land
Who said: Two vast and trunkless legs of stone
Stand in the desert. Near them on the sand,
Half sunk, a shatter'd visage lies, whose frown
And wrinkled lip and sneer of cold command
Tell that its sculptor well those passions read
Which yet survive, stamp'd on these lifeless things,
The hand that mock'd them and the heart that fed;
And on the pedestal these words appear:
'My name is Ozymandias, king of kings:
Look on my works, ye Mighty, and despair!'
Nothing beside remains. Round the decay
Of that colossal wreck, boundless and bare,
The lone and level sands stretch far away.

Percy Bysshe Shelley

from Metrical Feet

Lesson For A Boy

Trōchĕe trips frŏm lōng tŏ shŏrt;
From long to long in solemn sort
Slōw Spōndēe stālks; strōng fōot! yet ill able
Ēvĕr tŏ cōme ŭp wĭth Dāctўl trĭsўllăblĕ.
Ĭāmbĭcs mārch frŏm shŏrt tŏ lōng; –
Wĭth ă leāp ănd ă boūnd thĕ swĭft Ānăpăests thrōng;
One syllable long, with one short at each side,
Ămphībrăchўs hāstes wĭth ă stātelў stride; –
Fīrst ănd lāst bēĭng lōng, mĭddlĕ shŏrt, Ămphĭmācer
Strīkes hĭs thūndērĭng hoōfs like ă proūd high-brĕd Rācer.

Samuel Taylor Coleridge

All Day
It Has Rained

All day it has rained, and we on the edge of the moors
Have sprawled in our bell-tents, moody and dull
   as boors,
Groundsheets and blankets spread on the muddy
   ground
And from the first grey wakening we have found
No refuge from the skirmishing fine rain
And the wind that made the canvas heave and flap
And the taut wet guy-ropes ravel out and snap.
All day the rain has glided, wave and mist and dream,
Drenching the gorse and heather, a gossamer stream
Too light to stir the acorns that suddenly
Snatched from their cups by the wild south-westerly
Pattered against the tent and our upturned dreaming
   faces.
And we stretched out, unbuttoning our braces,
Smoking a Woodbine, darning dirty socks,
Reading the Sunday papers – I saw a fox
And mentioned it in the note I scribbled home; –
And we talked of girls and dropping bombs on Rome,
And thought of the quiet dead and the loud celebrities
Exhorting us to slaughter, and the herded refugees;
– Yet thought softly, morosely of them, and as indifferently
As of ourselves or those whom we
For years have loved, and will again
Tomorrow maybe love; but now it is the rain
Possesses us entirely, the twilight and the rain.

And I can remember nothing dearer or more to my heart
Than the children I watched in the woods on Saturday
Shaking down burning chestnuts for the schoolyard's
   merry play,
Or the shaggy patient dog who followed me
By Sheet and Steep and up the wooded scree
To the Shoulder o' Mutton where Edward Thomas
   brooded long
On death and beauty – till a bullet stopped his song.

Alun Lewis

Week Ending

It is Friday night in Bradford
The office girls are open wide
Legless in discos and wine bars
It is time for a bit on the side

They are spending money and laughing
While outside in the cold street
Little Alice plods to the Cathedral
She is eighty and slow on her feet

Her face is bound by a headscarf
She grimaces through rain and mist
Shuffling past the bright wine bars
Alice can't afford to get pissed

She gets her kicks from religion
Methodist, Catholic and Prod
It's not very warm in the churches
But the cold brings her nearer to God

Sheila has not yet seen thirty
But she's fat enough to have had kids
She's a cleaner at Social Security
Five nights a week on the skids

She smiles at girls dolled up brightly
They giggle and laugh at her socks
She wishes she could fit into hipsters
And her hair didn't look like a mop

On corners the newspaper sellers
Are dreaming of spirits and bitter
At seven they pack up their papers
And drift across town like litter

They must have names and addresses
They must have somewhere to go
They must have had other ambitions
Perhaps there is nothing to know

Inside the bright supermarket
The bachelors shop for themselves
They stare at women and children
Between the things on the shelves

At check-outs the shop-girls are hoping
For something better than this
Perhaps tonight at the disco
They'll get something more than a kiss

In Lumb Lane the night shift is forming
Standing on corners in pairs
In short skirts, jeans and leg-warmers
With cold eyes clocking the cars

The sky is dark blue like a sari
But the night is empty of stars
The streetlights mean something to someone
In the valley the red lights of cars

There's a man in the moon, tell the children
There's a man walking round City Hall
Just another week ending in Bradford
With another one waiting to fall.

March 1983

Jim Greenhalf

To a Friend on his Intended Marriage

Marriage, dear Mason, is a serious Thing;
'Tis proper every man should think it so;
'Twill either every human blessing bring,
Or load Thee with a settlement of woe.

Sometimes indeed it is a middle state,
Neither supremely blest, nor deeply cursed;
A stagnant pool of life, a dream of fate:
In my opinion, of all states the worst.

Thomas Chatterton

Thomas Chatterton died at the age of eighteen.

Things Shouldn't Be So Hard

A life should leave
deep tracks:
ruts where she
went out and back
to get the mail
or move the hose
around the yard;
where she used to
stand before the sink,
a worn-out place;
beneath her hand,
the china knobs
rubbed down to
white pastilles;
the switch she
used to feel for
in the dark
almost erased.
Her things should
keep her marks.
The passage
of a life should show;
it should abrade.
And when life stops,
a certain space
– however small –
should be left scarred
by the grand and
damaging parade.
Things shouldn't
be so hard.

Kay Ryan

Musée des Beaux Arts

About suffering they were never wrong,
The Old Masters: how well they understood
Its human position; how it takes place
While someone else is eating or opening a window or just
    walking dully along;
How, when the aged are reverently, passionately waiting
For the miraculous birth, there always must be
Children who did not specially want it to happen, skating
On a pond at the edge of the wood:
They never forgot
That even the dreadful martyrdom must run its course
Anyhow in a corner, some untidy spot
Where the dogs go on with their doggy life and the
    torturer's horse
Scratches its innocent behind on a tree.

In Breughel's *Icarus*, for instance: how everything turns
    away
Quite leisurely from the disaster; the ploughman may
Have heard the splash, the forsaken cry,
But for him it was not an important failure; the sun shone
As it had to on the white legs disappearing into the green
Water; and the expensive delicate ship that must have seen
Something amazing, a boy falling out of the sky,
Had somewhere to get to and sailed calmly on.

W. H. Auden

Summer Song I

I looked into my heart to write
  And found a desert there.
But when I looked again I heard
Howling and proud in every word
  The hyena despair.

Great summer sun, great summer sun,
  All loss burns in trophies;
And in the cold sheet of the sky
Lifelong the fish-lipped lovers lie
  Kissing catastrophes.

O loving garden where I lay
  When under the breasted tree
My son stood up behind my eyes
And groaned: Remember that the price
  Is vinegar for me.

Great summer sun, great summer sun,
  Turn back to the designer:
I would not be the one to start
The breaking day and the breaking heart
  For all the grief in China.

My one, my one, my only love,
  Hide, hide your face in a leaf,
And let the hot tear falling burn
The stupid heart that will not learn
  The everywhere of grief.

Great summer sun, great summer sun,
  Turn back to the never-never
Cloud-cuckoo, happy, far-off land
Where all the love is true love, and
  True love goes on for ever.

George Barker

Montana Born

I saw her first through wavering candlelight,
My sister in her cradle, one hour old;
Outside, the snow was drifting through the night,
But she lay warm, oblivious to the cold.

Her eyes were closed, the half-moist wisps of hair,
A honey harvest on her wrinkled head,
The smile upon her face as if she was elsewhere,
But knew the land she had inherited.

My mother there at peace, her labour done,
Their greyness gone, her cheeks were coralline,
She welcomed me, her wondering first-born son
And placed my sister's new-nailed hand in mine.

I looked out through the freezing window pane,
The whitening acres bare and stretching far
That nine months hence would heave with swelling grain,
And over every distant peak a star.

And she, my winter sister, does she know
That all this homely countryside is hers,
Where once were warring Sioux and buffalo,
And covered wagons full of travellers?

But I will tell her all the Indian tales,
And show her grass-high fields, and sugar beet,
We'll ride all day along the western trails,
Missouri River glinting at our feet.

Montana born, she'll sleep beneath these beams,
And learn the simple ways, and say her prayers,
And even now she may see in her dreams
Another boy come climbing up the stairs.

Leonard Clark

Report on Experience

I have been young, and now am not too old;
And I have seen the righteous forsaken,
His health, his honour and his quality taken.
This is not what we were formerly told.

I have seen a green country, useful to the race,
Knocked silly with guns and mines, its villages vanished,
Even the last rat and last kestrel banished –
God bless us all, this was peculiar grace.

I knew Seraphina; Nature gave her hue,
Glance, sympathy, note, like one from Eden.
I saw her smile warp, heard her lyric deaden;
She turned to harlotry; – this I took to be new.

Say what you will, our God sees how they run.
These disillusions are His curious proving
That he loves humanity and will go on loving;
Over there are faith, life, virtue in the sun.

Edmund Blunden

The Lovesleep

In an exciting world of love-bites, nipple-nipping,
unbuttoning and unzipping,
kisses that are
the highest kind of communication,
the lovers experience their timeless elation;

perhaps they reach those peaks where, like a bomb
    exploding,
the angels sing, encoding
ecstasies that
our language can never really deal with –
its nouns and its adjectives that no one can feel with;

but when the woman lies in the man's arms, soft,
sleeping,
in perfect trust, and keeping
faith, you might say,
that is the truest peace and disarming –
no one can sleep in the arms of an enemy, however
    charming.

Gavin Ewart

from *Tales of the Islands*

Chapter X

'adieu foulard…'

I watched the island narrowing the fine
Writing of foam around the precipices then
The roads as small and casual as twine
Thrown on its mountains; I watched till the plane
Turned to the final north and turned above
The open channel with the grey sea between
The fishermen's islets until all that I love
Folded in cloud; I watched the shallow green
That broke in places where there would be reef,
The silver glinting on the fuselage, each mile
Dividing us and all fidelity strained
Till space would snap it. Then, after a while
I thought of nothing, nothing, I prayed, would change;
When we set down at Seawell it had rained.

Derek Walcott

Upon Westminster Bridge

SEPT. 3, 1802

Earth has not anything to show more fair:
Dull would he be of soul who could pass by
A sight so touching in its majesty:
This City now doth like a garment wear

The beauty of the morning: silent, bare,
Ships, towers, domes, theatres, and temples lie
Open unto the fields, and to the sky,
All bright and glittering in the smokeless air.

Never did sun more beautifully steep
In his first splendour valley, rock, or hill;
Ne'er saw I, never felt, a calm so deep!

The river glideth at his own sweet will:
Dear God! the very houses seem asleep;
And all that mighty heart is lying still!

William Wordsworth

Junkie

The old suspension bridge was shaking.
The junkie on the rail was making
One last hazy calculation,
Climbed over, dropped his desperation
With his body. The grey river
Closed on thin flesh and thin shiver.
He had not thought there was a boat,
A boatman, looking for the float
Of life to save or drowned to gaff
Or some poor soul who's half and half
Glazed between heaven and earth to pump
Till the hushed heart begins to jump,
Or not. The lurking boatman caught
A splash, and shone his torch – fraught, fraught! –
Sighed as the almost weightless soul
Returned to find its casing whole
And the long struggle to divest
Illusion of its interest
Begun. Give him the saving grace
To set his second life in place!

Edwin Morgan

from The Deer's Cry

Saint Patrick's Breastplate

Today I put on
the sinews of the sky
flames of the sun
moon's glitter
fire's astonishment
lightning's strike
the power of the wind
ocean's trench
ungiving ground
solid rock

I call these powers to take my side
against every pitiless power
that seeks to stray my soul and body
against the chants of false prophets
against dark deeds of the gentiles
against the wrong-thinking of heretics
against sterile idolatry
against the spells of women, smiths and druids
against every mote of evil in man's body and soul.

Traditional: St Patrick

The Bloody Orkneys

This bloody town's a bloody cuss –
No bloody trains, no bloody bus,
And no one cares for bloody us –
    In bloody Orkney.

The bloody roads are bloody bad
The bloody folks are bloody mad,
They'd make the brightest bloody sad,
    In bloody Orkney.

All bloody clouds and bloody rains,
No bloody kerbs, no bloody drains,
The council's got no bloody brains
    In bloody Orkney.

Everything's so bloody dear,
A bloody bob for bloody beer,
And is it good? – no bloody fear
    In bloody Orkney.

The bloody flicks are bloody old,
The bloody seats are bloody cold,
You can't get in for bloody gold
    In bloody Orkney.

The bloody dances make you smile,
The bloody band is bloody vile,
It only cramps your bloody style,
    In bloody Orkney.

No bloody sport, no bloody games,
No bloody fun, the bloody dames
Won't even give their bloody names
        In bloody Orkney.

Best bloody place is bloody bed,
With bloody ice on bloody head,
You might as well be bloody dead,
        In bloody Orkney.

Traditional, recorded by Captain Hamish Blair

*Traditionally, the place name changes to anywhere the armed Forces
are staying.*

Praying to Big Jack

(for Ruthie, my God-child)

God, Jack of all trades,
I've got Ruthie's life to trade for today.
She's six. She's got her union card
and a brain tumor, that apple gone sick.
Take in mind, Jack, that her dimple
would erase a daisy. She's one of yours,
small walker of dogs and ice cream.
And she being one of yours
hears the saw lift off her skull
like a baseball cap. Cap off
and then what? The brains as
helpless as oysters in a pint container,
the nerves like phone wires.
God, take care, take infinite care
with the tumor lest it spread like grease.
Ruthie, somewhere in Toledo, has a twin,
mirror girl who plays marbles
and wonders: Where is the other me?
The girl of the same dress and my smile?
Today they sing together, they sing for alms.
God have you lapsed?
Are you so bitter with the world
you would put us down the drainpipe at six?

You of the top hat,
Mr God,
you of the Cross made of lamb bones,
you of the camps, sacking the rejoice out of Germany,

I tell you this . . .
it will not do.
I will run up into the sky and chop wood.
I will run to sea and find a thousand-year servant.
I will run to the cave and bring home a Captain
if you will only, will only,
dear inquisitor.

Banish Ruth, plump Jack,
and you banish all the world.

Anne Sexton

Poetry of Departures

Sometimes you hear, fifth-hand,
As epitaph:
*He chucked up everything
And just cleared off,*
And always the voice will sound
Certain you approve
This audacious, purifying,
Elemental move.

And they are right, I think.
We all hate home
And having to be there:
I detest my room,
Its specially-chosen junk,
The good books, the good bed,
And my life, in perfect order;
So to hear it said

He walked out on the whole crowd
Leaves me flushed and stirred,
Like *Then she undid her dress*
Or *Take that you bastard;*
Surely I can, if he did?
And that helps me stay
Sober and industrious.
But I'd go today,

Yes, swagger the nut-strewn roads,
Crouch in the fo'cs'le
Stubbly with goodness, if
It weren't so artificial,
Such a deliberate step backwards
To create an object:
Books; china; a life
Reprehensibly perfect.

Philip Larkin

On Meeting a Lady

It was surprising, after all the years,
To see how very little you had lost
Of all the things that made you, though one fears
You kept them somewhat to your cost.

To this sufficiency one had preferred
The faint uncertainties that lace a brow
Existence puzzled: if you had been stirred
By life, you must be different now.

No pathos of surrender, and no pride
Of winning have contributed their grace
To touch you: while the world has lived and died
No hint of this is in your face.

Only, intactness, a self-sheltered peace,
As if you would not let life have its say –
Poorer, I think, I find you now for these,
The things you would not cast away.

Charles L. O'Donnell

Love in a Bathtub

Years later we'll remember the bathtub,
the position
          of the taps
the water, slippery
as if a bucketful
          of eels had joined us . . .
we'll be old, our children grown up
but we'll remember the water
                    sloshing out
the useless soap,
the mountain of wet towels.
'Remember the bathtub in Belfast?'
we'll prod each other –

Sujata Bhatt

The Roman Centurion's Song

(Roman Occupation of Britain, AD 300)

Legate, I had the news last night, – my cohort ordered home
By ship to Portus Itius and thence by road to Rome.
I've marched the companies aboard, the arms are stowed
  below:
Now let another take my sword; Command me not to go!

I've served in Britain forty years, from Vectis to the Wall
I have none other home than this, nor any life at all.
Last night I did not understand, but, now the hour grows
  near
That calls me to my native land, I feel that land is here.

Here where men say my name was made, here where my
  work was done,
Here where my dearest dead are laid, my wife, my wife
  and son;
Here where time, custom, grief and toil, age, memory,
  service, love,
Have rooted me in British soil. Ah, how can I remove?

For me this land, that sea, these airs, those folk and fields
  suffice,
What purple Southern pomp can match our changeful
  Northern skies,
Black with December snows unshed, or pearled with
  August haze -
The clanging arch of steel-grey March, or June's long-
  lighted days?

You'll follow widening Rhodanus till vine and olive lean
Aslant before the sunny breeze that sweeps Nemausus
clean
To Arelate's triple gate; but let me linger on,
Here where our stiff-necked British oaks confront
Euroclydon.

You'll take the old Aurelian Road through shore-
descending pines
Where, blue as any peacock's neck, the Tyrrhene Ocean
shines.
You'll go where laurel crowns are won, but – will you
e'er forget
The scent of hawthorn in the sun, or bracken in the wet?

Let me work here for Britain's sake – at any task you will –
A marsh to drain, a road to make or native troops to drill.
Some Western camp (I know the Pict) or granite Border
keep,
'Mid seas of heather derelict, where our old messmates
sleep.

Legate, I come to you in tears – my cohort ordered home!
I've served in Britain forty years. What should I do in
Rome?
Here is my heart, my soul, my mind – the only life I know.
I cannot leave it all behind. Command me not to go!

Rudyard Kipling

Grief

I tell you, hopeless grief is passionless;
That only men incredulous of despair,
Half taught in anguish, through the midnight air
Beat upward to God's throne in loud access
Of shrieking and reproach. Full desertness
In souls as countries lieth silent-bare
Under the blanching, vertical eye-glare
Of the absolute heavens. Deep-hearted man, express

Grief for thy dead in silence like to death –
Most like a monumental statue set
In everlasting watch and moveless woe
Till itself crumble to the dust beneath.
Touch it; the marble eyelids are not wet.
If it could weep, it could arise and go.

Elizabeth Barrett Browning

from *The First Year*

The days fail: night broods over afternoon;
And at my child's first drink beyond the night
Her skin is silver in the early light.
Sweet the grey morning and the raiders gone.

E. J. Scovell

I Do Not Love Thee

I do not love thee! – no! I do not love thee!
And yet when thou art absent I am sad;
And envy even the bright blue sky above thee,
Whose quiet stars may see thee and be glad.

I do not love thee! – yet, I know not why,
Whate'er thou dost seems still well done, to me;
And often in my solitude I sigh
That those I do love are not more like thee!

I do not love thee! – yet, when thou art gone,
I hate the sound (though those who speak be dear)
Which breaks the lingering echo of the tone
Thy voice of music leaves upon my ear.

I do not love thee! – yet thy speaking eyes,
With their deep, bright and most expressive blue
Between me and the midnight heaven arise
Oftener than any eyes I ever knew.

I know I do not love thee! yet alas!
Others will scarcely trust my candid heart;
And oft I catch them smiling as they pass,
Because they see me gazing where thou art.

Caroline Elizabeth Sarah Norton

Those Winter Sundays

Sundays too my father got up early
and put his clothes on in the blueblack cold,
then with cracked hands that ached
from labour in the weekday weather made
banked fires blaze. No one ever thanked him.

I'd wake and hear the cold splintering, breaking.
When the rooms were warm, he'd call,
and slowly I would rise and dress,
fearing the chronic angers of that house,

Speaking indifferently to him,
who had driven out the cold
and polished my good shoes as well.
What did I know, what did I know
of love's austere and lonely offices?

Robert Hayden

Ye Wearie Wayfarer

Life is mostly froth and bubble.
Two things stand like stone.
Kindness in another's trouble,
Courage in your own.

Adam Lindsay Gordon

Kingsley Amis's version:

Life is mainly grief and labour.
Two things get you through.
Chortling when it hits your neighbour,
Whingeing when it's you.

Kingsley Amis

When the Glass of my Body Broke

Oh mother of sex,
lady of the staggering cuddle,
where do these hands come from?
A man, a Moby Dick of a man,
a swimmer going up and down in his brain,
the gentleness of wine in his fingertips,
where do these hands come from?
I was born a glass baby and nobody picked me up
except to wash the dust off me.
He has picked me up and licked me alive.

Hands
growing like ivy over me,
hands growing out of me like hair,
yet turning into fire grass,
planting an iris in my mouth,
spinning and blue,
the nipples turning into wings,
the lips turning into days that would not give birth,
days that would not hold us in their house,
days that would not wrap us in their secret lap,
and yet hands, hands growing out of pictures,
hands crawling out of the walls,
hands that excite oblivion,
like a wind,

a strange wind
from somewhere tropic
making a storm between my blind legs,
letting me lift the mask of the child from my face,
while all the toy villages fall
and I sink softly into
the heartland.

Anne Sexton

Let's Go Over It All Again

Some people are like that.
They split up and then they think:
Hey, maybe we haven't hurt each other to the uttermost.
Let's meet up and have a drink.

Let's go over it all again.
Let's rake over the dirt.
Let me pick that scab of yours.
Does it hurt?

Let's go over what went wrong –
How and why and when.
Let's go over what went wrong
Again and again.

We hurt each other badly once.
We said a lot of nasty stuff.
But lately I've been thinking how
I didn't hurt you enough.

Maybe there's more where that came from,
Something more malign.
Let me damage you again
For the sake of auld lang syne.

Yes, let me see you bleed again
For the sake of auld lang syne.

James Fenton

'Oh, oh, you will be sorry for that word!'

Oh, oh, you will be sorry for that word!
Give back my book and take my kiss instead.
Was it my enemy or my friend I heard,
'What a big book for such a little head!'
Come, I will show you now my newest hat,
And you may watch me purse my mouth and prink!
Oh, I shall love you still, and all of that.
I never again shall tell you what I think.
I shall be sweet and crafty, soft and sly;
You will not catch me reading any more:
I shall be called a wife to pattern by;
And some day when you knock and push the door,
Some sane day, not too bright and not too stormy,
I shall be gone, and you may whistle for me.

Edna St Vincent Millay

The Laboratory: Ancien Regime

Now that I, tying thy glass mask tightly,
May gaze thro' these faint smokes curling whitely,
As thou pliest thy trade in this devil's-smithy –
Which is the poison to poison her, prithee?

He is with her, and they know that I know
Where they are, what they do; they believe my tears flow
While they laugh, laugh at me, at me fled to the drear
Empty church, to pray God in, for them! – I am here.

Grind away, moisten and mash up thy paste,
Pound at thy powder, – I am not in haste!
Better sit thus and observe thy strange things
Than go where men wait me, and dance at the King's.

That in the mortar – you call it a gum?
Ah, the brave tree whence such gold oozings come!
And yonder soft phial, the exquisite blue,
Sure to taste sweetly, – is that poison too?

Had I but all of them, thee and thy treasures,
What a wild crowd of invisible pleasures!
To carry pure death in an earring, a casket,
A signet, a fan mount, a filigree basket!

Soon, at the King's, a mere lozenge to give,
And Pauline should have just thirty minutes to live!
But to light a pastille, and Elise, with her head,
And her breast, and her arms, and her hands, should
   drop dead!

Quick – is it finished? The colour's too grim!
Why not soft like the phial's, enticing and dim?
Let it brighten her drink, let her turn it and stir,
And try it and taste, ere she fix and prefer!

What a drop! She's not little, no minion like me!
That's why she ensnared him: this never will free
The soul from those masculine eyes, – say 'No!'
To that pulse's magnificent come-and-go.

For only last night, as they whispered, I brought
My own eyes to bear on her so, that I thought
Could I keep them one half-minute fixed, she would fall
Shrivelled; she fell not; yet this does it all!

Not that I bid you spare her the pain;
Let death be felt, and the proof remain;
Brand, burn up, bite into its grace –
He is sure to remember her dying face!

Is it done? Take my mask off! Nay, be not morose!
It kills her, and this prevents seeing it close:
The delicate droplet, my whole fortune's fee!
If it hurts her, beside, can it ever hurt me?

Now, take all my jewels, gorge gold to your fill,
You may kiss me, old man, on my mouth, if you will!
But brush this dust off me, lest horror it brings
Ere I know it – next moment I dance at the King's.

Robert Browning

The Unpredicted

The goddess Fortune be praised (on her toothed wheel
I have been mincemeat these several years)
Last night, for a whole night, the unpredictable
Lay in my arms, in a tender and unquiet rest –
(I perceived the irrelevance of my former tears) –
Lay, and at dawn departed. I rose and walked the streets
Where a whitsuntide wind blew fresh, and blackbirds
Incontestably sang, and the people were beautiful.

John Heath-Stubbs

Juliet

So come I into church again
My body straight as thunder rain
My mouth grey as sirocco skies.
My lids are newly fallen snow
And no March now will ever show
The tears that bloom inside my eyes.

Before the swift world turned to me
Before the green plain, like a sea,
Shouldering Verona wall
Pushed the stones and lizards down,
Unpicked the cobbles of the town,
I never touched the world at all.

Now high in church my father stands
And takes my father by the hands.
The living peal into the sun
United as a chime of bells
But in the dark, like scattered pearls,
The matchless dead lie, one by one.

Low on the bright mosaic floor
I who am Juliet no more
Have become Juliet at last,
Candlelit, unchangeable.
In this loud night the miracle
Of tomb and history goes past.

Patricia Beer

Shitty

Look thy last on all things shitty
While thou'rt at it: soccer stars,
Soccer crowds, bedizened bushheads
Jerking over their guitars.

German tourists, plastic roses,
Face of Mao and face of Che,
Women wearing curtains, blankets,
Beckett at the ICA,

High-rise blocks and action paintings,
Sculptures made from wire and lead:
Each of them a sight more lovely
Than the screens around your bed.

Kingsley Amis

Tramontana* at Lerici

Today, should you let fall a glass, it would
Disintegrate, played off with such keenness
Against the cold's resonance (the sounds
Hard, separate and distinct, dropping away
In a diminishing cadence) that you might swear
This was the imitation of glass falling.

Leaf-dapples sharpen. Emboldened by this clarity
The minds of artificers would turn prismatic
Running on lace perforated in crisp wafers
That could cut like steel. Constitutions
Drafted under this fecund chill, would be annulled
For the strictness of their equity, the moderation of their pity.

At evening, one is alarmed by such definition
In as many lost greens as one will give glances to recover,
As many again which the landscape
Absorbing into the steady dusk, condenses
From aquamarine to that slow indigo-pitch
Where the light and twilight abandon themselves.

And the chill grows. In this air
Unfit for politicians and romantics
Dark hardens from blue, effacing the windows:
A tangible block, it will be no accessory
To that which does not concern us. One is ignored
By so much cold suspended in so much night.

Charles Tomlinson

*tramontana – a cold mountain wind

On a Favourite Cat, Drowned in a Tub of Gold Fishes

'Twas on a lofty vase's side
Where China's gayest art had dyed
The azure flowers that blow,
Demurest of the tabby kind,
The pensive Selima reclined,
Gazed on the lake below.

Her conscious tail her joy declared:
The fair round face, the snowy beard,
The velvet of her paws,
Her coat that with the tortoise vies,
Her ears of jet, and emerald eyes—
She saw, and purr'd applause.

Still had she gazed, but 'midst the tide
Two angel forms were seen to glide,
The Genii of the stream:
Their scaly armour's Tyrian hue
Through richest purple, to the view
Betray'd a golden gleam.

The hapless Nymph with wonder saw:
A whisker first, and then a claw
With many an ardent wish
She stretch'd, in vain, to reach the prize—
What female heart can gold despise?
What Cat's averse to Fish?

Presumptuous maid! with looks intent
Again she stretch'd, again she bent,
Nor knew the gulf between—
Malignant Fate sat by and smiled—
The slippery verge her feet beguiled;
She tumbled headlong in!

Eight times emerging from the flood
She mew'd to every watery God
Some speedy aid to send:—
No Dolphin came, no Nereid stirr'd,
Nor cruel Tom nor Susan heard—
A favourite has no friend!

From hence, ye Beauties! undeceived
Know one false step is ne'er retrieved,
And be with caution bold:
Not all that tempts your wandering eyes
And heedless hearts, is lawful prize,
Not all that glisters, gold!

Thomas Gray

Encouragements to a Lover

Why so pale and wan, fond lover?
Prythee, why so pale?
Will, if looking well can't move her,
Looking ill prevail?
Prythee, why so pale?

Why so dull and mute, young sinner?
Prythee, why so mute?
Will, when speaking well can't win her,
Saying nothing do't?
Prythee, why so mute?

Quit, quit, for shame! this will not move,
This cannot take her;
If of herself she will not love,
Nothing can make her:
The D—l take her!

Sir John Suckling

Sampler

This is the sequence:
border, numbers, letters, name and date,
a thin, black motto for encouragement.

Learn simple stitches first (a slanting line, a cross,
arrangements of silk hyphens in long rows)
then fill the petals of rectangular flowers
sown on the pale grid of the cloth.

Make sure the back is neat, the stray ends cut.
There will be other places
for green, unravelling strands and knots of blood.

Adèle Geras

How the Wild South East Was Lost

For Robert Maclean

See, I was raised on the wild side, border country,
Kent 'n' Surrey, a spit from the county line,
An' they bring me up in a prep school over the canyon:
Weren't no irregular verb I couldn't call mine.

Them days, I seen oldtimers set in the ranch-house
(Talkin' bout J. 'Boy' Hobbs and Pat C. Hendren)
Blow a man clean away with a Greek optative,
Scripture test, or a sprig o that rho-do-dendron.

Hard pedallin' country, stranger, flint 'n' chalkface,
Evergreen needles, acorns an' beechmast shells,
But atop that old lone pine you could squint clean over
To the dome o' the Chamber o' Commerce in Tunbridge
    Wells.

Yep, I was raised in them changeable weather conditions:
I seen 'em, afternoon of a sunny dawn,
Clack up the deck chairs, bolt for the back French
    windows
When they bin drinkin' that strong tea on the lawn.

In a cloud o' pipesmoke rollin' there over the canyon,
Book-larned me up that Minor Scholarship stuff:
Bent my back to that in-between innings light roller
And life weren't easy. And that's why I'm so tough.

Kit Wright

Sun and Fun

I walked into the night-club in the morning;
There was kummel on the handle of the door.
The ashtrays were unemptied,
The cleaning unattempted,
And a squashed tomato sandwich on the floor.

I pulled aside the thick magenta curtains
– So Regency, so Regency, my dear –
And a host of little spiders
Ran a race across the ciders
To a box of baby 'pollies by the beer.

Oh sun upon the summer-going by-pass
Where everything is speeding to the sea,
And wonder beyond wonder
That here where lorries thunder
The sun should ever percolate to me.

When Boris used to call in his Sedanca,
When Teddy took me down to his Estate,
When my nose excited passion
When my clothes were in the fashion,
And my beaux were never cross if I was late,

There was sun enough for lazing upon beaches,
There was fun enough for far into the night.
But I'm dying now and done for,
What on earth was all the fun for?
For I'm old and ill and terrified and tight.

John Betjeman

Caustic Soda

The week the first baby died
my father visited –
awkward and lost in the new house
with stains on the floor
that would not fade.

While I was crying in hospital
he was on his knees,
not praying – scrubbing
with caustic soda and wire wool –
heedless for hours
with no gloves on.

He hid his red and bleeding hands –
said he hadn't felt the pain.
I held them gently, scolding,
not needing to say
that I'd learned how it feels
to love your child that way.

Liz Houghton

'They flee from me'

They flee from me that sometime did me seek,
With naked foot stalking in my chamber:
I have seen them gentle, tame and meek,
That now are wild, and do not remember
That sometime they put themselves in danger
To take bread at my hand; and now they range
Busily seeking with a continual change.

Thank't be Fortune, it hath been otherwise
Twenty times better; but once in special,
In thin array, after a pleasant guise,
When her loose gown from her shoulders did fall,
And she me caught in her arms long and small,
Therewith all sweetly did me kiss,
And softly said, 'Dear heart, how like you this?'

It was no dream; for I lay broad awaking:
But all is turned through my gentleness,
Into a strange fashion of forsaking;
And I have leave to go of her goodness;
And she also to use new-fangleness.
But since that I so kindly am served
I would fain know what she has deserved.

Sir Thomas Wyatt

A Bookshop Idyll

Between the GARDENING and the COOKERY
  Comes the brief POETRY shelf;
By the Nonesuch Donne, a thin anthology
  Offers itself.

Critical, and with nothing else to do,
  I scan the Contents page,
Relieved to find the names are mostly new;
  No one of my age.

Like all strangers, they divide by sex:
  Landscape Near Parma
Interests a man, so does *The Double Vortex*
So does *Rilke* and *Buddha*.

'I travel you see,' 'I think' and 'I can read'
  These titles seem to say;
But *I remember You, Love is my Creed,*
  Poem for J.,

The ladies' choice, discountenance my patter
  For several seconds;
For somewhere in this (as in any) matter
  A moral beckons.

Should poets bicycle-pump the human heart
  Or squash it flat?
Man's love is of man's life a thing apart;
  Girls aren't like that.

We men have got love well weighed up; our stuff
   Can get by without it.
Women don't seem to think that's good enough;
   They write about it,

And the awful way their poems lay them open
   Just doesn't strike them.
Women are really much nicer than men:
   No wonder we like them.

Deciding this, we can forget those times
   We sat up half the night
Chock-full of love, crammed with bright thoughts,
      names, rhymes,
   And couldn't write.

Kingsley Amis

from *The Sonnets*

116

Let me not to the marriage of true minds
Admit impediments. Love is not love
Which alters when it alteration finds,
Or bends with the remover to remove:
O, no! it is an ever-fixèd mark,
That looks on tempests and is never shaken;
It is the star to every wandering bark,
Whose worth's unknown, although his height be taken.
Love's not Time's fool, though rosy lips and cheeks
Within his bending sickle's compass come;
Love alters not with his brief hours and weeks,
But bears it out even to the edge of doom.
   If this be error and upon me proved,
   I never writ, nor no man ever loved.

William Shakespeare

Elizabethan Tragedy: A Footnote

That prudent Prince who ends Shakespearian plays
And wanders in to tell us how we wasted time
To hate or fall in love or be deranged
Would, three hours earlier, have ruined the play.
And so experience is, after all,
The heart of the matter. Even chatter
And babbling, or scenes in the worst of love affairs,
Like tears, or throwing things or being pushed downstairs
Have value in the long run. Caution has its place.
Premeditation though, I think, when face to face
With Sturm und Drang can never win the race.
Although the Prince is on the angels' side,
What got him there is wholesale homicide.

Howard Moss

Volcano and Iceberg

There will be an explosion one day,
This calm exterior will crack,
Seas will come up,
New islands,
New devastations.
This is me, this is me.

Sail round me, yachts, smacks, steamers,
Explorers come nearer,
Seven-eighths of me is below the surface.
One day, soon, that seven-eighths is coming to the top.

So beautiful I am
With my calm face
But I am cold to the touch,
I can also burn you,
I am saying something about stars and climates.
Soon the explosion is coming.
I don't want to be there then.

Elizabeth Jennings

Glass

Will not bleed
but wounds when itself wounded.
Outlives a generation, cracks
at a blow, sharp sound.
Older than the Pharaohs, bends
with furnace heat, polishes to ice surface,
screams at engraver's knife.
Backcloth for raindrops, frost crystals,
flying angels, saints in carmine,
all colours, and none,
will keep out angry voices, snow drifts.
Married to light, holds rainbows
in chandeliers, broken bottles, or show
delicate architecture of wasp's wing,
fault in bone, diamond;
can be a false jewel.
Glass gives new eyes, photographs of eyes,
prospects of life through an inch of it,
telescopes a dead star;
in league with sun will burn
forests and fields to loose ashes.
Milky, clear, solid as rock,
flowers to Venetian stem, gilt goblet,
hour glass on the run, bauble for Christmas,
dancing float, witches' ball.
The whole world is a house of glass;
we breathe our frail names on its cold face.

Leonard Clark

To Lucasta, on Going to the Wars

Tell me not, Sweet, I am unkind
That from the nunnery
Of thy chaste breast and quiet mind,
To war and arms I fly.

True, a new mistress now I chase,
The first foe in the field;
And with a stronger faith embrace
A sword, a horse, a shield.

Yet this inconstancy is such
As you too shall adore;
I could not love thee, Dear, so much,
Loved I not Honour more.

Richard Lovelace

Aristocrats

'I Think I am Becoming a God.'*

The noble horse with courage in his eye
clean in the bone, looks up at a shell burst:
away fly the images of the shires
but he puts the pipe back in his mouth.

Peter was unfortunately killed by an 88:
it took his leg away, he died in the ambulance.
I saw him crawling on the sand, he said:
It's most unfair; they've shot my foot off.

How can I live among this gentle
obsolescent breed of heroes, and not weep?
Unicorns almost,
for they are fading into two legends
in which their stupidity and chivalry
are celebrated. Each, fool and hero, will be an immortal.

These plains were their cricket pitch
and in the mountains the tremendous drop fences
brought down some of the runners. Here then
under the stones and earth they dispose themselves,
I think with their famous unconcern.
It is not gunfire I hear, but a hunting horn.

Keith Douglas

* *The dying Emperor Vespasian is supposed to have murmured, 'Alas, I think
I am about to become a god.'*

The Net

The net like a white vault, hung overhead
Dewy and glistening in the full moon's light,
Which cast a shadow-pattern of the thread
Over our face and arms, laid still and white
Like polished ivories on the dark bed.
The truck's low side concealed from us the sight
Of tents and bivouacs and track-torn sand
That lay without; only a distant sound
Of gunfire sometimes or, more close at hand,
A bomb, with dull concussion of the ground,
Pressed in upon our world, where, all else banned,
Our lonely souls eddied like echoing sound
Under the white cathedral of the net,
And like a skylark in captivity
Hung fluttering in the meshes of our fate,
With death at hand and, round, eternity.

Enoch Powell

Magnesium

It might as well be gaslight now
That soughs and pouches through the trees,
Lost pockets of foxed sepia,
The silver, pollen-haunted sneeze
Of sunshine and magnesium
Caught in the filter of her veil,
Uplifted faces drained and dumb,
Each smile a failing chemical
That hovers in the nitrate's mist
Where moth-like cousins, lunar aunts
In gauze and satin gloves persist
Through acid-eaten radiance.

There will be mustard-gas, morphine,
Candescent flash-backs, shell-burst skies,
Iron lamps whose phutterings sustain
Blown corpses' phosphorescent sighs,
But in the soft hiss of this flare,
Time stops to oxidise his face,
Shakes out behind her carboned stare
Annihilations of white lace,
As light implodes and leaves a husk,
A stiff, wing-collared, dried-up glow
Still holding back the brim of dusk
Where all their shining futures go.

John Levett

Lessons of the War

(*To Alan Michell*)

Vixi duellis nuper idoneus
Et militavi non sine gloria

1. NAMING OF PARTS

Today we have naming of parts. Yesterday,
We had daily cleaning. And tomorrow morning,
We shall have what to do after firing. But today,
Today we have naming of parts. Japonica
Glistens like coral in all of the neighbouring gardens,
    And today we have naming of parts.

This is the lower sling swivel. And this
Is the upper sling swivel, whose use you will see,
When you are given your slings. And this is the piling swivel,
Which in your case you have not got. The branches
Hold in the gardens their silent, eloquent gestures,
    Which in our case we have not got.

This is the safety-catch, which is always released
With an easy flick of the thumb. And please do not let me
See anyone using his finger. You can do it quite easy
If you have any strength in your thumb. The blossoms
Are fragile and motionless, never letting anyone see
    Any of them using their finger.

And this you can see is the bolt. The purpose of this
Is to open the breech, as you see. We can slide it
Rapidly backwards and forwards: we call this
Easing the spring. And rapidly backwards and forwards
The early bees are assaulting and fumbling the flowers:
    They call it easing the Spring.

They call it easing the Spring; it is perfectly easy
If you have any strength in your thumb; like the bolt,
And the breech, and the cocking-piece, and the point of
    balance,
Which in our case we have not got; and the almond-blossom
Silent in all of the gardens and the bees going backwards
    and forwards,
        For today we have naming of parts.

Henry Reed

Anthem for Doomed Youth

What passing-bells for these who die as cattle?
   Only the monstrous anger of the guns.
   Only the stuttering rifles' rapid rattle
Can patter out their hasty orisons.
No mockeries now for them; no prayers nor bells,
   Nor any voice of mourning save the choirs, –
The shrill, demented choirs of wailing shells;
   And bugles calling for them from sad shires.

What candles may be held to speed them all?
   Not in the hands of boys, but in their eyes
Shall shine the holy glimmers of good-byes.
   The pallor of girls' brows shall be their pall;
Their flowers the tenderness of patient minds,
And each slow dusk a drawing-down of blinds.

Wilfred Owen

Armistice

Snuff the candles, day is done,
Foeman scattered,
Battle won;
Blood ridged mountains of this morning
Solaced, shade the tiring sun.

Field to furrow,
Speed your cart;
Caesar's rendered,
Played your part;
Now in deep nostalgic stillness
Seek the voices of your heart.

Duty called for,
Paid with zest;
Hatred nourished,
Fought your best;
Now the man who slew his brother,
Homes to peace, but knows no rest.

Berlin, 1945

John Buxton Hilton

from *Fatal Interview*

Well, I have lost you fairly,
In my own way and with my full consent.
Say what you will, kings in a tumbril rarely
Went to their deaths more proud than this one went.
Some nights of apprehension and hot weeping
I will confess; but that's permitted me;
Day dried my eyes; I was not one for keeping
Rubbed in a cage a wing that would be free.
If I had loved you less or played you slyly
I might have held you for a summer more,
But at the cost of words I value highly,
And no such summer as this one before.
Should I outlive this anguish – and men do –
I shall have only good to say of you.

Edna St Vincent Millay

Ianthe

From you, little Ianthe, little troubles pass
Like little ripples down a sunny river;
Your pleasures spring like daisies in the grass,
Cut down, and up again as blithe as ever.

Walter Savage Landor

Unfortunate Coincidence

By the time you swear you're his,
    Shivering and sighing,
And he vows his passion is
    Infinite, undying –
Lady, make a note of this:
    One of you is lying.

Dorothy Parker

'It's the Season for Broken Hearts'

It's the season for broken hearts.
The trees in the park stripped bare,
The streets sordid
With old cans, broken bottles,
Yellowed newspapers reporting
Those glorious days last year
Before our fates collided.
We sit home and examine our hurts
To see if they are still hurting,
And wait for the phone call
That will resume our war –
Dominance and submission,
The silences of battle
As each waits for the other
To announce a new position.
Then a bird chirrups 'Why bother?'
On a branch no longer naked.
A stranger comes to the door
With the necessary gift of danger.

Edward Lucie-Smith

The Roach

A roach
came struttin
across my bedroom
floor,
like it was beyond
reproach,
or was
some sexy-lookin
whore,
and if I hadn't
snuffed it,
left it
alive,
I know it would've
come right up
and gave me
five!

John Raven

'Remember Now Thy Creator'

Remember now thy Creator in the days of thy youth,
while the evil days come not, nor the years draw nigh,
when thou shalt say, I have no pleasure in them;
While the sun, or the light, or the moon, or the stars, be
not darkened, nor the clouds return after the rain;
In the day when the keepers of the house shall tremble,
and the strong men shall bow themselves, and the
grinders cease because they are few, and those that
look out of the windows be darkened,
And the doors shall be shut in the streets, when the
sound of the grinding is low, and he shall rise up at the
voice of the bird, and all the daughters of musick shall
be brought low;

Also when they shall be afraid of that which is high, and
fears shall be in the way, and the almond tree shall
flourish, and the grasshopper shall be a burden, and
desire shall fail: because man goeth to his long home,
and the mourners go about the streets:
Or ever the silver cord be loosed, or the golden bowl be
broken, or the pitcher be broken at the fountain, or the
wheel broken at the cistern.

Then shall the dust return to the earth as it was: and the
spirit shall return unto God who gave it.

Ecclesiastes 12, The Bible

Portrait of a Young Girl
Raped at a Suburban Party

And after this quick bash in the dark
You will rise and go
Thinking of how empty you have grown
And of whether all the evening's care in front of mirrors
And the younger boys disowned
Led simply to this.

Confined to what you are expected to be
By what you are
Out in this frozen garden
You shiver and vomit –
Frightened, drunk among trees,
You wonder at how those acts that called for tenderness
Were far from tender.

Now you have left your titterings about love
And your childishness behind you
Yet still far from being old
You spew up among flowers
And in the warm stale rooms
The party continues.

It seems you saw some use in moving away
From that group of drunken lives
Yet already ten minutes pregnant
In twenty thousand you might remember
This party
This dull Saturday evening
When planets rolled out of your eyes
And splashed down in suburban grasses.

Brian Patten

To the Moon

Art thou pale for weariness
Of climbing heaven, and gazing on the earth,
Wandering companionless
Among the stars that have a different birth,–
and ever-changing, like a joyless eye
That finds no object worth its constancy?

Percy Bysshe Shelley

Broken Moon

(For Emma)

Twelve, small as six,
strength, movement, hearing
all given in half measure,
my daughter,
child of genetic carelessness,
walks uphill, always.

I watch her morning face;
precocious patience as she hooks each sock,
creeps it up her foot,
aims her jersey like a quoit.
My fingers twitch;
her private frown deters.

Her jokes can sting:
'My life is like dressed crab
– lot of effort, rather little meat.'
Yet she delights in seedlings taking root,
finding a fossil,
a surprise dessert.

Chopin will not yield to her stiff touch;
I hear her cursing.
She paces Bach exactly,
firm rounding of perfect cadences.
Somewhere inside
she is dancing a courante.

In dreams she skims the sand,
curls toes into the ooze of pools,
leaps on to stanchions.
Awake, her cousins take her hands;
they lean into the waves,
stick-child between curved sturdiness.

She turns away from stares,
laughs at the boy who asks
if she will find a midget husband.
Ten years ago, cradling her,
I showed her the slice of silver in the sky.
'Moon broken,' she said.

Carole Satyamurti

Walking Away

(For Sean)

It is eighteen years ago, almost to the day –
A sunny day with the leaves just turning,
The touch-lines new-ruled – since I watched you play
Your first game of football, then, like a satellite
Wrenched from its orbit, go drifting away

Behind a scatter of boys. I can see
You walking away from me towards the school
With the pathos of a half-fledged thing set free
Into a wilderness, the gait of one
Who finds no path where the path should be.

That hesitant figure, eddying away
Like a winged seed loosened from its parent stem,
Has something I never quite grasp to convey
About nature's give-and-take – the small, the scorching
Ordeals which fire one's irresolute clay.

I have had worse partings, but none that so
Gnaws at my mind still. Perhaps it is roughly
Saying what God alone could perfectly show –
How selfhood begins with a walking away,
And love is proved in the letting go.

C. Day Lewis

'Time does not being relief'

Time does not bring relief; you all have lied
Who told me time would ease me of my pain!
I miss him in the weeping of the rain;
I want him at the shrinking of the tide;
The old snows melt from every mountain-side,
And last year's leaves are smoke in every lane;
But last year's bitter loving must remain
Heaped on my heart, and my old thoughts abide.
There are a hundred places where I fear
To go, – so with his memory they brim.
And entering with relief some quiet place
Where never fell his foot or shone his face
I say, 'There is no memory of him here!'
And so stand stricken, so remembering him.

Edna St Vincent Millay

from Hamlet

(ACT III, SCENE I)

To be, or not to be; that is the question:
Whether 'tis nobler in the mind to suffer
The slings and arrows of outrageous fortune,
Or to take arms against a sea of troubles,
And, by opposing end them? To die: to sleep
No more; and, by a sleep to say we end
The heart-ache and the thousand natural shocks
That flesh is heir to, 'tis a consummation
Devoutly to be wished. To die, to sleep.
To sleep: perchance to dream: ay, there's the rub;
For in that sleep of death what dreams may come
When we have shuffled off this mortal coil,
Must give us pause. There's the respect
That makes calamity of so long life;
For who would bear the whips and scorns of time,
The oppressor's wrong, the proud man's contumely,
The pangs of disprized love, the law's delay,
The insolence of office, and the spurns
That patient merit of the unworthy takes,
When he himself might his quietus make
With a bare bodkin? Who would these fardels bear,
To grunt and sweat under a weary life,
But that the dread of something after death,
The undiscovered country from whose bourn
No traveller returns, puzzles the will,
And makes us rather bear those ills we have
Than fly to others that we know not of?
Thus conscience does make cowards of us all . . .

William Shakespeare

Adam Talks to the Press

He made a garden. Laid it out for me.
And then He filched my rib. Fixed me a mate.
For years, we mooched about and that was great.
We found the Snake was quite good company.
After a bite of that sweet apple-fruit,
I knew some things I never used to know:
how much we needed clothes. How parts that show
are better covered. Next stop: fig-leaf suit.
But when the Maker saw us, He went spare
and chucked us out, and forced the Snake to crawl,
but I think this: He *knew* that we would fall.
That Tree of Knowledge needn't have been there.
He could have planted anything instead:
roses, carnations, a magnolia tree,
but no, He needed her and me
to crunch that apple and jump into bed.
A flaming sword stood in the Angel's hand
as we left Paradise. *So* OTT.
Eve started crying, natch, but as for me,
I was resigned. The whole thing had been planned.
Now, looking back, how blissful it all seems!
The blossoming, the flowers and the green,
the fountains and the shade. We could have been
contented there forever. In your dreams!

Adèle Geras

One Poet Visits Another

His car was worth a thousand pounds and more,
A tall and glossy black silk hat he wore;
His clothes were pressed, like pretty leaves, when they
Are found in Bibles closed for many a day;
Until the birds I love dropped something that –
    As white as milk, but thick as any cream –
Went pit, pit, pat! Right on his lovely hat!

Lead this unhappy poet to his car –
    Where is his longing now, where his desire?
When left alone, I'll ride him to his grave,
    On my own little horse of wind and fire.

W. H. Davies

If I Could Tell You

Time will say nothing but I told you so,
Time only knows the price we have to pay;
If I could tell you I would let you know.

If we should weep when clowns put on their show,
If we should stumble when musicians play,
Time will say nothing but I told you so.

There are no fortunes to be told, although,
Because I love you more than I can say,
If I could tell you I would let you know.

The winds must come from somewhere when they blow,
There must be reasons why the leaves decay;
Time will say nothing but I told you so.

Perhaps the roses really want to grow,
The vision seriously intends to stay;
If I could tell you I would let you know.

Suppose the lions all get up and go,
And all the brooks and soldiers run away;
Will Time say nothing but I told you so?
If I could tell you I would let you know.

W. H. Auden

She Writes Her First Poem

Nothing remarkable. A lisp on paper.
Perfectly spelled; the scansion adequate
Provided you work out which words to lean on.

She keeps no record of the thing itself
But later may recall that it began
'Oh how I wish I had . . .' A knocking bet;
She is a calculating little girl.

Later she will not call to mind the words
Much less the subject. But the praise, the praise!
The tilted heads, moist eyes and steepled hands,
The implication that she had 'done well'.
And the reward; the gentle revelation
That being read is being listened-to.

This is her first taste of the subtle joy
Of writing down something she dare not say
So as to pass it, like a folded note,
From a safe place behind a grown-up's chair.

Her mother has it still, though God knows where.

Ann Drysdale

To Someone Who Insisted
I Look Up Someone

from *Japanese Beetles*

I rang them up while touring Timbuctoo,
Those bosom chums to whom you're known as '*Who?*'

X. J. Kennedy

I Am

I am! yet what I am who cares or knows?
    My friends forsake me like a memory lost.
I am the self-consumer of my woes;
    They rise and vanish, an oblivious host,
Shadows of life, whose very soul is lost.
And yet I am – I live though I am toss'd

Into the nothingness of scorn and noise,
    Into the living sea of waking dreams,
Where there is neither sense of life, nor joys,
    But the huge shipwreck of my own esteem
And all that's dear. Even those I loved the best –
Are strange – nay, they are stranger than the rest.

I long for scenes where man has never trod;
    For scenes where woman never smiled or wept;
There to abide with my Creator, GOD,
    And sleep as I in childhood sweetly slept:
Full of high thoughts, unborn. So let me lie,
– The grass below – above the vaulted sky.

John Clare

from *Last Poems*

Tell me not here, it needs not saying,
   What tune the enchantress plays
In aftermaths of soft September
   Or under blanching mays,
For she and I were long acquainted
   And I knew all her ways.

On russet floors, by waters idle,
   The pine lets fall its cone;
The cuckoo shouts all day at nothing
   In leafy dells alone;
And travellers' joy beguiles in autumn
   Hearts that have lost their own.

On acres of the seeded grasses
   The changing burnish heaves;
Or marshalled under moons of harvest
   Stand still at night the sheaves;
Or beeches strip in storms for winter
   And stain the wind with leaves.

Possess, as I possessed a season,
   The countries I resign,
Where over elmy plains the highway
   Would mount the hills and shine,
And full of shade the pillared forest
   Would murmur and be mine.

For nature, heartless, witless nature,
    Will neither care nor know
What stranger's feet may find the meadow
    And trespass there and go,
Nor ask amid the dews of morning
    If they are mine or no.

A. E. Housman

Western Wind When Wilt Thou Blow

Western wind when wilt thou blow
the small rain down can rain
Christ if my love were in my arms
and I in my bed again

Anon (early 16th century)

Snow

The room was suddenly rich and the great bay-window was
Spawning snow and pink roses against it
Soundlessly collateral and incompatible:
World is suddener than we fancy it.

World is crazier and more of it than we think,
Incorrigibly plural. I peel and portion
A tangerine and spit the pips and feel
The drunkenness of things being various.

And the fire flames with a bubbling sound for world
Is more spiteful and gay than one supposes –
On the tongue on the eyes on the ears in the palms of
    one's hands –
There is more than glass between the snow and the huge
    roses.

Louis MacNeice

Dover Beach

The sea is calm to-night.
The tide is full, the moon lies fair
Upon the straits; – on the French coast the light
Gleams and is gone; the cliffs of England stand,
Glimmering and vast, out in the tranquil bay.
Come to the window, sweet is the night-air!
Only, from the long line of spray
Where the sea meets the moon-blanch'd land,
Listen! you hear the grating roar
Of pebbles which the waves draw back, and fling,
At their return, up the high strand,
Begin, and cease, and then again begin,
With tremulous cadence slow, and bring
The eternal note of sadness in.

Sophocles long ago
Heard it on the Aegean, and it brought
Into his mind the turbid ebb and flow
Of human misery; we
Find also in the sound a thought,
Hearing it by this distant northern sea.

The Sea of Faith
Was once, too, at the full, and round earth's shore
Lay like the folds of a bright girdle furl'd.
But now I only hear
Its melancholy, long, withdrawing roar,
Retreating, to the breath
Of the night-wind, down the vast edges drear
And naked shingles of the world.

Ah, love, let us be true
To one another! for the world, which seems
To lie before us like a land of dreams,
So various, so beautiful, so new,
Hath really neither joy, nor love, nor light,
Nor certitude, nor peace, nor help for pain;
And we are here as on a darkling plain
Swept with confused alarms of struggle and flight,
Where ignorant armies clash by night.

Matthew Arnold

Summer Beach

For how long known this boundless wash of light,
    This smell of purity, this gleaming waste,
This wind? This brown, strewn wrack how old a sight,
    These pebbles round to touch and salt to taste.

See, the slow marbled heave, the liquid arch,
    Before the waves' procession to the land
Flowers in foam; the ripples' onward march,
    Their last caresses on the pure hard sand.

For how long known these bleaching corks, new-made
    Smooth and enchanted from the lapping sea?
Since first I laboured with a wooden spade
    Against this background of Eternity.

Frances Cornford

The Frog Prince

He was cold as slime,
Coloured to the underside
Of a rotted leaf
Mottled brown and yellow.

With promises of princehood underneath
The skin – if warmed by love –
He chose my pillow
For his transformation,
Croaked at me to stroke his throat
Pulsing like a swamp-bubble.

Pity froze to contempt;
Rather than touch him I lifted the pillow,
Flung him into the night.
Now alone in autumn mood I wonder
Who is this tall young man
Supple as willow and wind,
Carrying the sun on his shoulder.
His light shafts through me to its mark
In a girl not beautiful but kind.

Phoebe Hesketh

Mid-Term Break

I sat all morning in the college sick bay
Counting bells knelling classes to a close.
At two o'clock our neighbours drove me home.

In the porch I met my father crying –
He had always taken funerals in his stride –
And Big Jim Evans saying it was a hard blow.

The baby cooed and laughed and rocked the pram
When I came in, and I was embarrassed
By old men standing up to shake my hand

And tell me they were 'sorry for my trouble'.
Whispers informed strangers I was the eldest,
Away at school, as my mother held my hand

In hers and coughed out angry tearless sighs,
At ten o'clock the ambulance arrived
With the corpse, stanched and bandaged by the nurses.

Next morning I went up into the room. Snowdrops
And candles soothed the bedside; I saw him
For the first time in six weeks. Paler now,

Wearing a poppy bruise on his left temple,
He lay in the four-foot box as in his cot.
No gaudy scars, the bumper knocked him clear.

A four-foot box, a foot for every year.

Seamus Heaney

My Little Lize

Who is de prutties' gal you say?
Oh, hush up man an go away.
Yo don't know w'at yo talkin bout;
Yo ought to go an fin' dat out.
De prutties' gal dat one can meet
Dat ever walk along de street;
I guess yo never seen my Lize;
If yo had seen her – bless yo eyes,
Yo would be sure to 'gree wid me,
Dat she's de sweetes' gal dat be.
Why man! where was yo all dis time,
Dat yo don't see dis gal of mine?
Her skin is black an smoode as silk;
Her teet' is jus' as white as milk;
Her hair is of dem fluffy kin',
Wid curls a-hanging, black an shine.
Her shape is such dat can't be beat;
So graceful, slender an so neat.
W'ene'er she turn her eyes on you,
Dey seem to strike yo t'rough an t'rough,
Dere's not a sweeter lookin face;
An lips dat mek you feel to tas'e.
Her hands is small an so's her feet,
Wid such a pair of enkles neat!
W'en she goes out to tek a walk
She sets de people all to talk.
De gals dey envy her wid fear,
Dey feel so cheap we'en she is near.
De boys de lif' dere hats an try
To win a smile as she pass by.

But w'at's de use o talkin' so;
An try such beauty here to show!
Yo better see wid yo own eyes
Dis sweet an lovely little Lize;
For if I try de evening t'rough,
I couldn't quite explain to you.

James Martinez

Our Hold on the Planet

We asked for rain. It didn't flash and roar.
It didn't lose its temper at our demand
And blow a gale. It didn't misunderstand
And give us more than our spokesman bargained for,
And just because we owned to a wish for rain,
Send us a flood and bid us be damned and drown.
It gently threw us a glittering shower down.
And when we had taken that into the roots of grain,
It threw us another, and then another still
Till the spongy soil again was natal wet.
We may doubt the just proportion of good to ill.
There is much in nature against us. But we forget:
Take nature altogether since time began,
Including human nature, in peace and war,
And it must be a little more in favour of man,
Say a fraction of one per cent at the very least,
Or our number living wouldn't be steadily more,
Our hold on the planet wouldn't have so increased.

Robert Frost

The Sunlight on the Garden

The sunlight on the garden
Hardens and grows cold,
We cannot cage the minute
Within its nets of gold,
When all is told
We cannot beg for pardon.

Our freedom as free lances
Advances towards its end;
The earth compels, upon it
Sonnets and birds descend;
And soon, my friend,
We shall have no time for dances.

The sky was good for flying
Defying the church bells
And every evil iron
Siren and what it tells:
The earth compels,
We are dying, Egypt, dying

And not expecting pardon,
Hardened in heart anew,
But glad to have sat under
Thunder and rain with you,
And grateful too
For sunlight on the garden.

Louis MacNeice

Charles

He was born blind with the snow on a winter's day;
The moon blank as marble stared at him from the full,
But his mother wept to see the vacant rolling of his eyes;
His father dared not look and despairingly turned away
When hands like feelers fumbled in space to pull
Fingers and lips to upturned face to recognize.
Growing older he sat in the dark learning voices by heart,
Carried on conversations with birds singing in summer
  trees,
Heard brooks changing their sound at floodtime, the
  angled dart
Of dazzled bats diving through twilight air.
But music played by wandering band or organ at the fair
Moved him to tears and fingers to invisible keys,
So that at twenty-five he began to drown the village church
With ceaseless tides of Handel, Bach and Mendelssohn,
And magnified the Lord for seven-and-thirty years.
With egg-shaped head he sat upright upon his perch.
Praying on flute we might depart in peace,
Triumphant came from Egypt on the bombardon,
Made thunderstorms at will, stars race like charioteers,
Captivity to turn, the harvest to increase;
He brought sweet healing to the troubled mind,
Fearlessly opened the eyes of the blind.

Leonard Clark

Rising Five

'I'm rising five,' he said,
'Not four,' and little coils of hair
Un-clicked themselves upon his head.
His spectacles, brimful of eyes to stare
At me and the meadow, reflected cones of light
Above his toffee-buckled cheeks. He'd been alive
Fifty-six months or perhaps a week more:

                                        not four,
But rising five.

Around him in the field the cells of spring
Bubbled and doubled; buds unbuttoned; shoot
And stem shook out the creases from their frills,
And every tree was swilled with green.
It was the season after blossoming,
Before the forming of the fruit:

                              not May,
But rising June.

                                  And in the sky
The dust dissected the tangential light:

                                    not day,
But rising night;
                  not now,
But rising soon.

The new buds push the old leaves from the bough.
We drop our youth behind us like a boy
Throwing away his toffee-wrappers. We never see the
    flower,
But only the fruit in the flower; never the fruit,
But only the rot in the fruit. We look for the marriage bed
In the baby's cradle, we look for the grave in the bed:
                                                        not living,
But rising dead.

Norman Nicholson

Next, Please

Always too eager for the future, we
Pick up bad habits of expectancy.
Something is always approaching; every day
Till then we say,

Watching from a bluff the tiny, clear,
Sparkling armada of promises draw near.
How slow they are! And how much time they waste,
Refusing to make haste!

Yet still they leave us holding wretched stalks
Of disappointment, for, though nothing balks
Each big approach, leaning with brasswork prinked,
Each rope distinct,

Flagged, and the figurehead with golden tits
Arching our way, it never anchors; it's
No sooner present than it turns to past.
Right to the last

We think each one will heave to and unload
All good into our lives, all we are owed
For waiting so devoutly and so long.
But we are wrong:

Only one ship is seeking us, a black-
Sailed unfamiliar, towing at her back
A huge and birdless silence. In her wake
No waters breed or break.

Philip Larkin

Hush-a-bye, Baby

All right, dear, I'll not risk bad dreams again
For our small daughter, singing her to sleep
With my sad ballads. Now Sir Patrick Spens
Can stay dry-shod; Queen Jane shall not cry out
For Good King Henry in her agony;
The channering worm shall chide no more; fair Janet
Must leave her true-love to the elf-queen's keeping,
And Arlen's wife will absolutely not
Be pinned right through the heart against the wall.
Henceforth, as you request, I shall confine myself,
Like any normal dad, to nursery rhymes:
Strange egg-shaped characters will smash themselves
Irreparably; ill-housed, harassed mothers
Whip hungry children; babies fall from trees;
Mice shall be maimed; sheep lost; arachnophobes
Fare badly; innocent domestics suffer
Sudden nasectomies, and at the end
We shall dance rosy-faced in a ring and drop dead with
    the plague.

In either case, outside the small lit bedroom
The glass shall weep with rain, the winds be howling
Their old, uncensorable savageries.
But you are right, of course: we should choose well
What songs we sing, to lull them for a while.

David Sutton

from *Merciless Beauty*

Your eyen two will slay me suddenly;
I may the beauty of them not sustain,
So woundeth it throughout my hearte keen.

And but your word will healen hastily
My hearte's wounde, while that it is green,
Your eyen two will slay me suddenly;
I may the beauty of them not sustain.

Upon my truth I say you faithfully
That ye bin of my life and death the queen;
For with my death the truthe shall be seen.
   Your eyen two will slay me suddenly;
   I may the beauty of them not sustain,
   So woundeth it throughout my hearte keen.

Geoffrey Chaucer

To His Coy Mistress

Had we but world enough, and time,
This coyness, Lady, were no crime
We would sit down and think which way
To walk and pass our long love's day.
Thou by the Indian Ganges' side
Should'st rubies find: I by the tide
Of Humber would complain. I would
Love you ten years before the Flood,
And you should, if you please, refuse
Till the conversion of the Jews.
My vegetable love should grow
Vaster than empires, and more slow.
An hundred years should go to praise
Thine eyes and on thy forehead gaze;
Two hundred to adore each breast,
But thirty thousand to the rest.
An age at least to every part,
And the last age should show your heart.
For, Lady, you deserve this state,
Nor would I love at lower rate.
    But at my back I always hear
Time's wingèd chariot hurrying near;
And yonder all before us lie
Deserts of vast eternity.
Thy beauty shall no more be found,
Nor, in my marble vault, shall sound
My echoing song: then worms shall try
That long preserved virginity,

And your quaint honour turn to dust,
And into ashes all my lust.
The grave's a fine and private place,
But none, I think, do there embrace.
    Now therefore, while the youthful hue
Sits on thy skin like morning dew,
And while thy willing soul transpires
At every pore with instant fires,
Now let us sport us while we may,
And now, like amorous birds of prey,
Rather at once our time devour
Than languish in his slow-chapt power.
Let us roll all our strength and all
Our sweetness up into one ball,
And tear our pleasures with rough strife
Through the iron gates of life:
Thus, though we cannot make our sun
Stand still, yet we will make him run.

Andrew Marvell

Roger Bavidge

Not for his curly mop and freckled nose,
his concertina socks and scabby knees,
nor for his cleverness, but just because
he was my sort of person, I suppose,
I felt this tenderness, but could not name
my feeling at that time. I was too young,
   but Shakespeare could have named it,
   Shakespeare knew
   a thing or two of love.

And we were sitting talking, side by side
on the high vaulting-horse, when someone said
'Is Roger your fiancé?' I denied
that I had any feelings, though I had,
and afterwards disguised my tenderness
with scorn, like Beatrice insulting Ben
   four hundred years ago, for Shakespeare knew
   a thing or two of love.

I mocked his curly mop and freckled nose,
his concertina socks and scabby knees;
though I was scruffy too, I mocked his clothes.
We were ten or eleven, I suppose.
'Your socks are full of holes, your shirt is ripped;
why doesn't someone mend them?' Roger wept.
   Benedick could answer blow for blow,
   but Roger Bavidge, forty years ago,
   knew something even Shakespeare could not know.

Our teacher told me later: 'Roger cried
because, six months ago, his mother died.'
Never again did we sit side by side
discussing this and that. I should have tried
to make amends for being such a savage
to one who was my friend. Dear Roger Bavidge,
    do you remember me? And do you know
    what Shakespeare knew four hundred years ago?

Anna Adams

Les Sylphides

Life in a day: he took his girl to the ballet;
Being shortsighted himself could hardly see it –
    The white skirts in the grey
    Glade and the swell of music
    Lifting the white sails.

Calyx upon calyx, Canterbury bells in the breeze
The flowers on the left mirror to the flowers on the right
    And the naked arms above
    The powdered faces moving
    Like seaweed in a pool.

Now, he thought, we are floating – ageless, oarless –
Now there is no separation, from now on
    You will be wearing white
    Satin and a red sash
    Under the waltzing trees.

But the music stopped, the dancers took their curtain,
The river had come to a lock – a shuffle of programmes –
    And we cannot continue down
    Stream unless we are ready
    To enter the lock and drop.

So they were married – to be the more together –
And found they were never again so much together,
    Divided by the morning tea,
    By the evening paper,
    By children and tradesmen's bills.

Waking at times in the night she found assurance
Due to his regular breathing but wondered whether
It was really worth it and where
The river had flowed away
And where were the white flowers.

Louis MacNeice

Lost Days

Then, when an hour was twenty hours, he lay
Drowned under grass. He watched the carrier ant,
With mandibles as trolley, push in front
Wax-yellow specks across the parched cracked clay.
A tall sun made the stems down there transparent.
Moving, he saw the speedwell's sky blue eye
Start up next to his own, a chink of sky
Stamped deep through the tarpaulin of a tent.
He pressed his mouth against the rooted ground.
Held in his arms, he felt the earth spin round.

Stephen Spender

Abbey Tomb

I told them not to ring the bells
The night the Vikings came
Out of the sea and passed us by.
The fog was thick as cream
And in the abbey we stood still
As if our breath might blare
Or pulses rattle if we once
Stopped staring at the door.

Through the walls and through the fog
We heard them passing by.
The deafer monks thanked God too soon
And later only I
Could catch the sound of prowling men
Still present in the hills
So everybody else agreed
To ring the abbey bells.

And even while the final clang
Still snored upon the air,
And while the ringers joked their way
Down round the spiral stair,
Before the spit of fervent prayer
Had dried into the stone
The raiders came back through the fog
And killed us one by one.

Father Abbot at the altar
Lay back with his knees
Doubled under him, caught napping
In the act of praise.
Brother John lay unresponsive
In the warming room.
The spiders came out for the heat
And then the rats for him.

Under the level of the sheep
Who graze here all the time
We lie now, under tourists' feet
Who in good weather come.
I told them not to ring the bells
But centuries of rain
And blustering have made their tombs
Look just as right as mine.

Patricia Beer

The Mother

Of course I love them, they are my children.
That is my daughter and this is my son.
And this is my life I give them to please them.
It has never been used. Keep it safe. Pass it on.

Anne Stevenson

Oh! Death Will Find Me

Oh! Death will find me, long before I tire
   Of watching you; and swing me suddenly
Into the shade and loneliness and mire
   Of the last land! There, waiting patiently,

One day, I think, I'll feel a cool wind blowing,
   See a slow light across the Stygian tide,
And hear the Dead about me stir, unknowing,
   And tremble. And I shall know that you have died,

And watch you, a broad-browed and smiling dream,
   Pass, light as ever, through the lightless host,
Quietly ponder, start, and sway, and gleam –
   Most individual and bewildering ghost!

And turn, and toss your brown delightful head
Amusedly, among the ancient Dead.

Rupert Brooke

from *More Poems*

I did not lose my heart in summer's even,
When roses to the moonlight burst apart;
When plumes were under heel and lead was flying,
In blood and smoke and flame I lost my heart.

I lost it to a soldier and a foeman,
A chap that did not kill me, but he tried;
That took the sabre straight and took it striking,
And laughed and kissed his hand to me and died.

A. E. Housman

In the Queen's Room

In smoky outhouses of the court of love
I chattered, a recalcitrant underling
Living on scraps. 'Below stairs or above,
All's one,' I said. 'We valets have our fling.'

Now I am come, by a chance beyond reach,
Into your room, my body smoky and soiled
And on my tongue the taint of chattering speech,
Tell me, Queen, am I irredeemably spoiled?

Norman Cameron

Burning of the Exeter Theatre

'Twas in the year of 1887, which many people will long
   remember,
The burning of the Theatre at Exeter on the 5th of
   September,
Alas! that ever-to-be-remembered and unlucky night,
When one hundred and fifty lost their lives, a most
   agonising sight.

The play on this night was called 'Romany Rye',
And at act four, scene third, Fire! Fire! was the cry;
And all in a moment flames were seen issuing from the
   stage,
Then the women screamed frantically, like wild beasts in
   a cage.

Then a panic ensued, and each one felt dismayed,
And from the burning building a rush was made;
And soon the theatre was filled with a blinding smoke,
So that the people their way out had to grope.

The shrieks of those trying to escape were fearful to hear,
Especially the cries of those who had lost their friends
   most dear;
Oh, the scene was most painful in the London Inn Square,
To see them wringing their hands and tearing their hair!

And as the flames spread, great havoc they did make,
And the poor souls fought heroically in trying to make
   their escape;
Oh, it was horrible to see men and women trying to reach
   the door!
But in many cases death claimed the victory, and their
   struggles were o'er.

Alas! 'twas pitiful the shrieks of the audience to hear,
Especially as the flames to them drew near;
Because on every face were depicted despair and woe,
And many of them jumped from the windows into the
    street below.

The crushed and charred bodies were carried into
    London Hotel yard,
And to alleviate their sufferings the doctors tried
    hard;
But, alas! their attendance on many was thrown away,
But those that survived were conveyed to Exeter Hospital
    without delay.

And all those that had their wounds dressed proceeded
    home,
Accompanied by their friends, and making a loud
    moan;
While the faces and necks of others were sickening to
    behold,
Enough to chill one's blood, and make the heart turn
    cold.

Alas! words fail to describe the desolation,
And in many homes it will cause great lamentation;
Because human remains are beyond all identification,
Which will cause the relatives of the sufferers to be in
    great tribulation.

Oh, Heaven! it must have been an awful sight,
To see the poor souls struggling hard with all their
    might,
Fighting hard their lives to save,
While many in the smoke and burning flame did madly
    rave!

It was the most sickening sight that ever anybody saw,
Human remains, beyond recognition, covered with a
  heap of straw;
And here and there a body might be seen, and a maimed
  hand,
Oh, such a sight, that the most hard-hearted person could
  hardly withstand!

The number of the people in the theatre was between
  seven and eight thousand,
But, alas! one hundred and fifty by the fire have been
  found dead;
And the most lives were lost on the stairs leading from
  the gallery,
And these were roasted to death, which was sickening to
  see.

The funerals were conducted at the expense of the local
  authority,
And two hours and more elapsed at the mournful
  ceremony;
And at one grave there were two thousand people, a very
  great crowd,
And most of the men were bareheaded and weeping aloud.

Alas! many poor children have been bereft of their
  fathers and mothers,
Who will be sorely missed by little sisters and brothers;
But, alas! unto them they can ne'er return again,
Therefore the poor little innocents must weep for them in
  vain.

I hope all kind Christian souls will help the friends of the
  dead,
Especially those that have lost the winners of their bread;
And if they do, God surely will them bless,
Because pure Christianity is to help the widows and
  orphans in distress.

I am very glad to see Henry Irving has sent a hundred
  pounds,
And I hope his brother actors will subscribe their mite all
  round;
And if they do it will add honour to their name,
Because whatever is given towards a good cause they
  will it regain.

William McGonagall

also known as 'the World's Worst Poet'

The Exchange

We pledged our hearts, my love and I –
   I in my arms the maiden clasping;
I could not guess the reason why,
   But oh! I trembled like an aspen.

Her father's love she bade me gain;
   I went, but shook like any reed!
I strove to act the man – in vain!
   We had exchanged our hearts indeed.

Samuel Taylor Coleridge

Say Not the Struggle
Naught Availeth

Say not the struggle naught availeth,
The labour and the wounds are vain,
The enemy faints not, nor faileth,
And as things have been they remain.

If hopes were dupes, fears may be liars;
It may be, in yon smoke conceal'd,
Your comrades chase e'en now the fliers,
And, but for you, possess the field.

For while the tired waves, vainly breaking,
Seem here no painful inch to gain,
Far back, through creeks and inlets making,
Comes silent, flooding in, the main.

And not by eastern windows only,
When daylight comes, comes in the light;
In front the sun climbs slow, how slowly!
But westward, look, the land is bright!

Arthur Hugh Clough

Release

For years, he'd grown and blocked out all the light,
stretched and expanded to fill up her space.
He turned his face away from her at night.
His eyes were small stones in a stiffened face.
Someone she did not fully recognize,
whose words were metal scraping in her ears
sat at the table in his special chair,
while she drank water to wash down the tears
she never shed. Now everything had changed.
Around her head she sensed the high, blue air.
After the funeral, she'd rearranged
the things that she no longer had to share:

the furniture, the ornaments, her mind,
her bedroom and her heart. Oh, Death was kind!

Adèle Geras

I is a Long Memoried Woman

From dih pout
of mi mouth
from dih
treacherous
calm of mih
smile
you can tell

I is a long memoried woman

Grace Nichols

Poetry

And it was at that age . . . Poetry arrived
in search of me. I don't know, I don't know where
it came from, from winter or a river.
I don't know how or when,
no, they were not voices, they were not
words, nor silence,
but from a street I was summoned,
from the branches of night,
abruptly from the others,
among violent fires
or returning alone,
there I was without a face
and it touched me.

I did not know what to say, my mouth
had no way
with names,
my eyes were blind,
and something started in my soul,
fever or forgotten wings,
and I made my own way,
deciphering
that fire,
and I wrote the first faint line,
faint, without substance, pure
nonsense,
pure wisdom
of someone who knows nothing,
and suddenly I saw
the heavens
unfastened

and open,
planets,
palpitating plantations,
shadow perforated,
riddled
with arrows, fire and flowers,
the winding night, the universe.

And I, infinitesimal being,
drunk with the great starry
void,
likeness, image of
mystery,
felt myself a pure part
of the abyss,
I wheeled with the stars,
my heart broke loose on the wind.

Pablo Neruda

The Apparition

When by thy scorne, O murdresse, I am dead,
And that thou thinkst thee free
From all solicitation from mee,
Then shall my ghost came to thy bed,
And thee, fain'd vestal, in worse armes shall see;
Then thy sicke taper will begin to winke,
And he, whose thou art then, being tyr'd before,
Will, if thou stirre, or pinch to wake him, thinke
    Thou call'st for more,
And in false sleepe will from thee shrinke,
And then poore Aspen wretch, neglected thou
Bath'd in a cold quicksilver sweat wilt lye
    A veryer ghost than I;
What I will say, I will not tell thee now,
Lest that preserve thee; and since my love is spent,
I had rather thou shouldst painfully repent,
Than by my threatenings rest still innocent.

John Donne

The Sunne Rising

> Busie old foole, unruly Sunne,
> Why dost thou thus,
> Through windows, and through curtains call on us?
> Must to thy motions lovers seasons run?
> Sawcy pedantique wretch, goe chide
> Late schoole boyes and sowre prentices,
> Goe tell Court-huntsmen, that the King will ride,
> Call countrey ants to harvest offices;
> Love, all alike, no season knowes, nor clime,
> Nor houres, dayes, moneths, which are the rags of time.
>
> Thy beames, so reverend, and strong
> Why shouldst thou thinke?
> I could eclipse and cloud them with a winke,
> But that I would not lose her sight so long:
> If her eyes have not blinded thine,
> Looke, and to morrow late, tell mee,
> Whether both the'India's of spice and Myne
> Be where thou leftst them, or lie here with mee.
> Aske for those Kings whom thou saw'st yesterday,
> And thou shalt heare, All here in one bed lay.
>
> She'is all States, and all Princes, I,
> Nothing else is.
> Princes doe but play us; compar'd to this,
> All honor's mimique; All wealth alchimie.
> Thou sunne art halfe as happy as wee,
> In that the world's contracted thus;
> Thine age askes ease, and since they duties bee
> To warme the world, that's done in warming us.
> Shine here to us, and thou art every where;
> This bed thy center is, these walls, thy spheare.

John Donne

When You Are Old

When you are old and grey and full of sleep,
And nodding by the fire, take down this book,
And slowly read, and dream of the soft look
Your eyes had once, and of their shadows deep;

How many loved your moments of glad grace,
And loved your beauty with love false or true,
But one man loved the pilgrim soul in you,
And loved the sorrows of your changing face;

And bending down beside the glowing bars,
Murmur, a little sadly, how Love fled
And paced upon the mountains overhead
And hid his face amid a crowd of stars.

W. B. Yeats

On First Looking into Chapman's Homer*

Much have I travell'd in the realms of gold,
   And many goodly states and kingdoms seen;
   Round many western islands have I been
Which bards in fealty to Apollo hold.
Oft of one wide expanse had I been told
   That deep-brow'd Homer ruled as his demesne;
   Yet did I never breathe its pure serene
Till I heard Chapman speak out loud and bold:
Then felt I like some watcher of the skies
   When a new planet swims into his ken;
Or like stout Cortez when with eagle eyes
   He star'd at the Pacific – and all his men
Look'd at each other with a wild surmise –
   Silent, upon a peak in Darien.

John Keats

*George Chapman translated the Greek poet, Homer, into English

Index of Titles/First Lines

Index of Poets

Acknowledgements

The publishers and the compiler thank the following for permission to reprint copyright material:

Anna Adams, 'Roger Bavidge' from *Swings and Shadows*, edited by Anne Harvey (Julia McCrae Books, 1996), copyright © Anna Adams, 1995; reprinted by permission of the author.

Kingsley Amis, 'A Bookshop Idyll' from *A Case of Samples 1946–56* (Gollancz, 1956), copyright Kingsley Amis, 1956; 'Shitty' from *Collected Poems 1944–1979* (Hutchinson, 1979), copyright © Kingsley Amis, 1979; 'Ye Wearie Wayfarer' from *Experience* by Martin Amis (HarperCollins, 2000), poem copyright © Kingsley Amis, 2000; all reprinted by kind permission of Jonathan Clowes Ltd, London, on behalf of the Literary Estate of Sir Kingsley Amis.

W. H. Auden, 'Musée des Beaux Arts' and 'If I Could Tell You' from *Collected Poems* (Faber and Faber, 1976), copyright © Edward Mendelson, William Meredith and Monroe K. Spears, executors of the Estate of W. H. Auden, 1976; reprinted by permission of Faber and Faber.

George Barker, 'Summer Song 1' from *Collected Poems* (Faber and Faber, 1987), copyright © George Barker, 1987; reprinted by permission of Faber and Faber.

Patricia Beer, 'Abbey Tomb' from *Collected Poems* (Carcanet Press, 1988), copyright © Patricia Beer, 1967; 'Juliet' from *Loss of the Magyar* (Longmans Green, 1959), copyright © Patricia Beer, 1959; reprinted by permission of Carcanet Press Ltd.

John Betjeman, 'Sun and Fun' from *Collected Poems* (John Murray, 1958), copyright © John Betjeman, 1958, 1962, 1970; reprinted by permission of John Murray.

Sujata Bhatt, 'Love in a Bathtub' from *Point No Point* (Carcanet Press, 1997), copyright © Sujata Bhatt, 1997; reprinted by permission of Carcanet Press Ltd.

Edward Blunden, 'Report on Experience' from *Near and Far* (Cobden Sanderson, 1929), copyright © Edmund Blunden, 1929; reprinted by permission of Peters, Fraser and Dunlop Ltd on behalf of the Estate of Mrs Claire Blunden.

Edwin Brock, 'Song of the Battery Hen' from *Song of the Battery Hen* (Secker & Warburg, 1977), copyright © Edwin Brock, 1977; reprinted by permission of David Higham Associates Ltd.

Norman Cameron, 'In the Queen's Room' (Three Love Poems) from *Collected Poems* (Anvil Press, 1990), copyright © Jane Aiken Hodge, 1990; reprinted by permission of Jane Aiken Hodge.

G. K. Chesterton, 'The Rolling English Road' from *Collected Poems of G. K. Chesterton* (Methuen, 1933); reprinted by permission of A. P. Watt Ltd on behalf of the Royal Literary Fund.

Meng Chiao, 'Impromptu' from *Poems of the Late T'ang*, translated by A. C. Graham (Penguin, 1965), translation copyright © A. C. Graham, 1965; reprinted by permission of Penguin Books Ltd.

Leonard Clark, 'Glass' from *Collected Poems and Verses for Children* (Dobson Books Ltd, 1973), copyright © Leonard Clark, 1973; 'Charles' from *English Morning and Other Poems* (Hutchinson, 1953), copyright © Leonard Clark, 1953; 'Montana Born' from *The Broad Atlantic* (Dobson Books Ltd, 1974), copyright © Leonard Clark, 1974; all reprinted by permission of the Literary Executor of Leonard Clark.

Frances Cornford, 'Summer Beach' from *Selected Poems*, edited by Jane Dowson (Enitharmon Press, 1996), copyright © the Trustees of the Mrs F. C. Cornford Deceased Will Trust, 1996; reprinted by permission of Professor James Cornford for the Trustees of the Mrs F. C. Cornford Deceased Will Trust.

W. H. Davies, 'One Poet Visits Another' from *Complete Poems of W. H. Davies* (Jonathan Cape, 1963), copyright © Jonathan Cape Ltd, 1963; reprinted by permission of the Mrs H.

Kennedy, 1961, 1969, 1970, 1971; reprinted by permission of Curtis Brown Ltd.

Rudyard Kipling, 'The Roman Centurion's Song' from *The Works of Rudyard Kipling* (Wordsworth Poetry Library, 1994); reprinted by permission of A. P. Watt Ltd on behalf of the National Trust for Places of Historical Interest or Natural Beauty.

Philip Larkin, 'Poetry of Departures' and 'Next, Please' from *The Less Deceived* (Marvell Press, 1955); reprinted by permission of the Marvell Press, England and Australia.

Alun Lewis, 'All Day It Has Rained' from *Collected Poems* (Seren, 1994), copyright © the Estate of Alun Lewis, 1994; reprinted by permission of Seren.

Edward Lucie-Smith, '*It's the season for broken hearts ...*' from *Changing Shape: New and Selected Poems* (Carcanet Press, 2002), copyright © Edward Lucie-Smith, 2002; reprinted by permission of Carcanet Press Ltd.

Louis MacNeice, 'Snow', 'The Sunlight on the Garden' and 'Les Sylphides' from *Collected Poems* (Faber and Faber, 1966), copyright © the Estate of Louis MacNeice, 1966; reprinted by permission of David Higham Associates Ltd.

Edna St Vincent Millay, '*Time does not bring relief*', '*Oh, oh, you will be sorry*' and XLVII from *Fatal Interview* from *Selected Poems*, ed. Colin Falck (Carcanet Press, 1992), copyright © the Estate of Norma Millay Ellis, 1991; reprinted by permission of Carcanet Press Ltd.

Edwin Morgan, 'Junkie' first published in the *London Review of Books*, 22 June 2000, copyright © Edwin Morgan, 2000; reprinted by permission of Carcanet Press Ltd.

Howard Moss, 'Elizabethan Tragedy: A Footnote' from *A Swim off the Rocks* (Athenaeum, 1976), copyright © Howard Moss, 1976; reprinted by permission of Richard Evans.

Pablo Neruda, 'Poetry' from *Selected Poems*, translated by Alastair Reid (Jonathan Cape, 1970), translation copyright © Alastair Reid, 1970; reprinted by permission of The Random House Group Ltd.

Grace Nichols, '*I is a long memoried woman*' from *I Is a Long Memoried Woman* (Karnak House, 1983), copyright © Grace Nichols, 1983; reprinted by permission of Curtis Brown Ltd, London, on behalf of Grace Nichols.

Norman Nicholson, 'Rising Five' from *Collected Poems* (Faber and Faber, 1994), copyright © Irvine Hunt, 1994; reprinted by permission of David Higham Associates.

Dorothy Parker, 'Unfortunate Coincidence' from *The Collected Dorothy Parker*, copyright Dorothy Parker, 1926, renewed 1954; reprinted by permission of Gerald Duckworth & Co. Ltd.

Brian Patten, 'Portrait of a Young Girl Raped at a Suburban Party' from *Grinning Jack* (HarperCollins, 1995), copyright © Brian Patten, 1990; reprinted by permission of the author c/o Rogers, Coleridge and White Ltd, 11 Powys Mews, London W11 1JN.

Enoch Powell, 'The Net' from *Dancer's End* (Falcon Press, 1951), copyright © Enoch Powell, 1951; reprinted by permission of the J. Enoch Powell Literary Trust.

Alison Prince, 'Loss' first published in the *Literary Review*, 1999, copyright © Alison Prince, 1999; reprinted by permission of the Jennifer Luithlen Agency.

D. A. Prince, 'The Magi' first published in *Without Boundaries* (Manifold, 2001), copyright © D. A. Prince, 2001; reprinted by permission of the author.

Henry Reed, 'Naming of Parts' from *Lessons of the War* from *Collected Poems* edited by Jon Stallworthy (Oxford University Press, 1991); reprinted by permission of Oxford University Press.

Theodore Roethke, 'Lines upon Leaving a Sanitarium' from *Collected Poems* (Faber and Faber, 1968), copyright © Beatrice Roethke, 1968; reprinted by permission of Faber and Faber.

Kay Ryan, 'Things Shouldn't Be So Hard' first published in the *New Yorker*, 4 June 2001, copyright © Kay Ryan, 2001; reprinted by permission of the author.

Carole Satyamurti, 'Broken Moon' from *Selected Poems* (Bloodaxe Books, 2000), copyright © Carole Satyamurti, 2000; reprinted by permission of Bloodaxe Books.

Dennis Scott, 'Epitaph' from *Uncle Time* (University of Pittsburgh Press, 1973), copyright © Dennis Scott, 1973; reprinted by permission of the University of Pittsburgh Press.

E. J. Scovell, 'Days Drawing In' from *Collected Poems* (Carcanet Press, 1988), copyright © E.

J. Scovell, 1988; reprinted by permission of Carcanet Press Ltd.

Anne Sexton, 'Praying to Big Jack' and 'When the Glass of my Body Broke' from Anne *Sexton: The Complete Poems* (Houghton Mifflin, 1981), copyright © Linda Gray Sexton and Loring Conant Jr, executors of the will of Anne Sexton, 1981; reprinted by permission of Peters, Fraser and Dunlop Ltd on behalf of Anne Sexton.

Stephen Spender, 'Lost Days' from *The Generous Days* (Faber and Faber, 1971), copyright © Stephen Spender, 1971; reprinted by permission of Faber and Faber.

James Stephens, 'Nora Criona' from *Collected Poems* (Macmillan, 1926), copyright © James Stephens, 1926; reprinted by permission of the Society of Authors as the Literary Representative of the Estate of James Stephens.

Anne Stevenson, 'The Mother' from *The Collected Poems 1955–1995* (Bloodaxe Books, 2000), copyright © Anne Stevenson, 2000; reprinted by permission of Bloodaxe Books.

David Sutton, 'Hush-a-bye, Baby' from *Settlements* (Peterloo Poets, 1982), copyright © David Sutton, 1982; reprinted by permission of Peterloo Poets.

Charles Tomlinson, 'Tramontana at Lerici' from *Selected Poems* (Carcanet), copyright © Charles Tomlinson; reprinted by permission of Carcanet Press Ltd.

Derek Walcott, 'Chapter X: Tales of the Islands' from *Selected Poetry* (Heinemann, 1993), copyright © Derek Walcott, 1962; reprinted by permission of Faber and Faber and Farrah, Straus and Giroux.

Sylvia Townsend Warner, 'Azreal' from *Twelve Poems* (Chatto and Windus, 1980), copyright © Susanna Pinney and William Maxwell, 1980; reprinted by permission of The Random House Group Ltd.

Kit Wright, 'How the Wild South East Was Lost' from *Short Afternoons* (Hutchinson, 1989), copyright © Kit Wright, 1989; reprinted by permission of the author.

W. B. Yeats, 'When You Are Old' from *Collected Poems* (Macmillan, 1983), copyright © Michael Yeats, 1983; reprinted by permission of A. P. Watt on behalf of Michael Yeats.

Every effort has been made to trace the copyright holders of poems included in this anthology, but in some cases this has not proved possible. The publishers therefore wish to thank the authors or copyright holders of those poems which are included without acknowledgement above. The publishers would be grateful to be notified of any errors or omissions in the above list and will be happy to make good any such errors or omissions in future printings.